An Insider's Guide to Italy: Travel Tips, Tidbits, and Tales

By
Bruna A. Riccobon

Cover Art by Giordano Riccobon

Edited by Melissa Haas

All rights reserved.
Copyright © *2012* by Bruna A. Riccobon

All rights reserved. No part of this book may be reproduced in whole or in part without written permission from the publisher or author, except by reviewers who may quote brief excerpts in a newspaper, magazine, or electronic format; nor may any part of this book be reproduced, stored in a retrieval system, or transmitted in any form or by any means electronic, mechanical, photocopying, recording, or other, without written permission from Bruna A. Riccobon.

ISBN-13: 978-1-4776-1166-1
ISBN-9: 1-4776-1166-5

Updated November 2013

Table of Contents

Introduction
Before You Go: Pre-Trip Planning (p. 2)
When to Travel 3
Where to Go 4
Documents 5
Money, Credit Cards & Banking 9
Healthcare & Travel Insurance 14
Packing 16
Electronics, Phones & Other Equipment . 21

Getting There (p. 24)
Traveling With Young Children or Pets 30

Once You Have Arrived (p. 32)
Accommodations 32
   Types of Accommodations 32
   Defining Requirements 36
   Checking In 41
Italian Bathrooms 42
Elevators 48
Trains & The Italian Rail System 49
   Tickets, Passes & Reservations 53
   Luggage Handling 59
   Station Facilities 61
   Train Safety 63
Traveling Intercity
   Via Bus 66
   Driving 67
   Chauffeured Car 69
Getting Around the City 70
   Buses & Streetcars 70
   Taxis 72

Getting Around the City (cont'd)
  Subways & Funiculars 73
  Boats 74
Dining (Courses, Menus, Etc.) 77
  Hours, Credit Cards, Tipping 86
  Water & Other Beverages 88
Entertainment 95
  Casinos 97
  Sports 98
  Television 101
  Sight Seeing 102
Shopping (Areas & Goods) 104
  What You Can Bring Home 114
  Taxes 115
  Store Hours 116
Mailing & Shipping 117
Laundry 120
Safety 121
Language Barrier 126
Etiquette & The Italian Way Of Life 129
  Dress Codes & Customs 134

APPENDIX

Italian Legal Holidays, Months of the Year,
  Days of the Week 138
Types of Shops 139
Shoe and Clothing Sizes 140
Useful Words & Phrases 141

INTRODUCTION

My desire to see the world began as a toddler in war torn Italy. My grandfather, Nonno Marcello, used to read stories to us. It was during the height of World War II and television was still a dream. In the evening, when we weren't being bombarded, we sat around the big, wooden kitchen table, while my grandfather entertained us with adventure stories set in exotic places: the Casbah, Borneo, and the Wild West. I was fascinated by those tales and their locales; I looked forward to becoming an adult, when I could visit these places.

My first adventure took place much sooner than that. In 1951, when I was ten, I emigrated with my family from Trieste, Italy to Pittsburgh, Pennsylvania via refugee camps in Naples, Italy and Bremerhaven, Germany. The November train ride through the Swiss Alps, with its glistening snow, sparkling lakes and tiny cottages tucked in the mountains further stimulated my desire to see the world.

I have traveled extensively throughout the United States, Europe and South America. Over the past forty years, I have visited thirty-one countries and twenty-five states. I have taught a course on traveling in Italy, and during the last ten years, I have spent many months living and traveling there.

This book includes a collection of tips and stories; information that can be acquired only by experience. In short, what I wish I had known when I initially set out.

BEFORE YOU GO: PRE-TRIP PLANNING

The first thing you must decide is if you want to be part of a guided tour or venture out on your own. I am not a fan of guided tours; I find them too restrictive. Your entire life is planned and free time is at a premium. There's little room to experience the country, interact with the people and sample the local cuisine. There are a few tours that allow an adequate amount of free time and give travelers some opportunity to choose their own food, but I still find them too confining. The only exception is small, custom designed tours of twenty people or less.

If your sole goal is to check off the must-see sights, eat American-style food, and have little contact with the locals, then a guided tour is for you. I know a couple who has been to Europe over twenty times and has never tasted Italian gelato, a piece of Austrian torte or a real pizza. They've visited all the sights and bought a lot of souvenirs, but haven't really experienced any of the countries they visited.

I have gone on cruises to places where it was more convenient and cheaper to do so. Although I enjoyed them, they were not as memorable as when I traveled independently.

I've often traveled alone, but have never felt lonely and have met many interesting people. I have to admit that I have an advantage, since I speak Italian fluently, but I've also gone solo to countries where I don't understand more than two words. These days, when the majority of the service people speak English, exploring Europe is not so scary--even for a woman traveling alone. A friend, who has taken both guided tours and traveled freelance with me, admits that our trips were more relaxed and memorable.

The information in this guide should help alleviate the nxiety of traveling independently.

WHEN TO TRAVEL

I usually prefer to travel in what the travel industry calls "shoulder" season--April, May or September, October. These periods occur between the busy, crowded high season (June, July and August), and the less expensive (except for the Christmas and New Year's rates) low season (November through March).

Shoulder season is great because, although April and September can sometimes be wet, the temperature is comfortable overall and destinations are less crowded as students are still in school, and air fares and hotel rates are cheaper. If traveling in September, try to book your hotel early because many businesses and other organizations schedule their conventions during that month.

Travel during high season (June through August) is hectic. Summers in the southern half of Italy can be terribly humid and as hot as Dante's Inferno, especially in the inner cities. August is the worst month to travel, especially if you're headed anywhere near a resort destination. That's when the Northern Europeans descend on Italy, and Italians escape to the mountains and sea shore. Many restaurants and stores are closed; highways, trains and busses are overcrowded.

The advantages of traveling during low season (November through March) are that the crowds are gone; airfares and accommodations are cheaper--unless you're going to a ski resort or traveling around the Christmas holidays. In the southern part of Italy, winters are mild (temperatures similar to those of the Carolinas), but can be wet. Winters in certain parts of the north can be cold, humid and windy; snow occurs primarily in the mountains.

Exercise common sense in scheduling your trip around major holidays. A complete list of holidays is included at the back of this book (Appendix, p. 138).

WHERE TO GO

Most tourists visiting Italy head for the Big Three: Rome, Florence, and Venice because that's where most of the history, architecture, and art can be found. If you want to fully experience Italian culture and meet the locals, don't limit yourself to those famous destinations. You won't find the real Italy there. Many of the people you will encounter in those cities may be other tourists or expatriates. Recently, I've discovered that even the hotels and restaurants are now no longer staffed by Italians.

On my last trip to Florence, the hotel check-in clerk was Russian, the porter was Senegalese, and the maid, who didn't speak anything I understood, was from somewhere in Eastern Europe. The fellow who tried to sell me a leather jacket at the outdoor market was Chinese, and when the young Hungarian waiter in the quaint little restaurant realized I was Italian-American, he switched to English because he said his English was better than his Italian. I've had similar experiences in other major cities.

In the last couple of decades, the larger cities have attracted many foreign workers along with the hordes of tourists who visit every year. So, if you want to experience the real Italy and mingle with the locals, venture into the less touristy towns.

Just like in the United States, Italy's culture, food, and dialects vary from region to region. Every area has its own appeal, unique attractions, and culinary specialties. Even if your time in Italy is limited, try to include at least one or two of the lesser known destinations. If you're in Florence, add Lucca, Siena or San Gimignano to your itinerary. From Rome, take a train to the nearby ruins of Ostia Antica, or to Pompei, and Positano. Go east to the beaches of Senigallia or the lovely little medieval town of Corinaldo in the Marche region. Travel to Spoleto, where one of Europe's leading art festivals is held every summer.

When in Venice, take the train northwest to Vicenza with its Palladian architecture, or east to Trieste where you can sit in the main square and watch the sun set on the Adriatic. Visit Milan with its intricate Duomo, and glass-domed galleria—one of the first indoor shopping malls in the country; and then travel to one of the picturesque lakes that are located only a short train ride away. Travel to glamorous San Remo on the Italian Riviera, where the annual music festival is held, then visit the quaint little towns of the Cinque Terre area. Go to the parks and mountains of Val D'Aosta in the northwest, or to the ski resorts of the northeast.

Visit the ancient ruins of Pompeii, and then take a ride up the mountains to Sorrento. From there, take a hydrofoil to the enchanting isle of Capri.

Venture to the heel of the Italian boot, where you will find the town of Alberobello, famous for its unusual circular buildings with conical roofs called *trulli,* and the city of Taranto, home of the Tarantella. Travel to Sicily to see the golden *duomo* of Monreale and the picturesque town of Taormina, and if you like clear, blue waters, head for the glamorous beaches of Costa Smeralda in Sardinia.

Italy has sights and activities for all tastes and pocketbooks. Be adventurous and don't limit yourself to three cities when there are so many other places to visit.

DOCUMENTS

The most important item you need to have when traveling to a foreign country is a valid passport. Normally it only takes two or three weeks to process one, but I would recommend **allowing as much time as possible (at least a month, three months if possible), especially if you were born outside of the United States.**

~

Getting my first passport turned out to be a nightmare. I had allowed almost three months, which I thought was ample time, but I was wrong. In the seventies, you were required to provide at least three docu-

ments showing who you were, and when and where you were born. In my case, one of those had to be my naturalization paper.

Since my birth certificate was lost during the war, the only official document I had identifying me was a certificate of baptism provided by the diocese of Trieste. The document included my name, where and when I was born, as well as the names of my parents. Unfortunately, the clerk at the passport office was reluctant to accept it, especially because it was written in Italian.

"Is this an official birth certificate?" the clerk asked while looking at the thin, yellowed paper with the diocesan seal.

I made the mistake of telling the truth. "No, this is not a birth certificate; it's a baptismal certificate." In retrospect, I realized it would have been better if I had lied.

I explained to her about the war, how the documents were lost, and how the baptismal certificate was the only document I had. I reassured her that it was considered a valid document and had been previously accepted as such by other government agencies.

Her expression was somewhere between "I don't believe you," and "I could lose my job if I get this wrong."

"I don't know. We normally only accept birth certificates," she said scrutinizing it once more. "Don't you have anything in English?"

I was getting testy. I was on my lunch hour and hadn't eaten yet.

"How could I have something in English when I was born in Italy?"

"I'll have to ask my supervisor. He's not available right now, so I'll have to call you back."

I waited patiently for several days, but never received a call. One week later, I returned to the passport office and learned that the document had been deemed acceptable. I thought my problems were over, but I was wrong.

I had been told that the processing would take a maximum of six weeks, but by the time ten weeks had elapsed, I still didn't have a passport. I called the office and, after several days of contacting various departments, discovered there was a record of my application but nothing else. Someone had "misplaced" all the documents I had attached to the application.

"When were you planning to inform me of this?" I asked the clerk who had told me about the missing attachments. She didn't have a satisfactory answer.

I had to contact relatives in Italy and ask them to send me a new copy of the certificate of baptism. I also had to go through the process of getting new naturalization papers.

My passport finally arrived two days prior to my departure. date. This experience isn't exactly the normal one, although I had a friend who didn't have a driver's license go through similar problems and delays.

~

Today's technology helps expedite the process, but allow plenty of time if you're applying for your first passport, and if you don't receive it within a month, contact the passport office.

If you are planning to stay in Italy for more than ninety days, you will need to get a permit, which can be obtained at the police headquarters (*questura*) in the city where you will be residing, at a U.S. consulate, or an Italian consulate in the U.S. prior to departure. The permit is usually granted routinely to U.S. citizens.

There's another important matter that is often overlooked: **A divorced parent who is planning to take his or her children to a foreign country must get a letter signed by his/her ex-spouse giving permission to take such children abroad.** This applies to any minor under eighteen years of age traveling with anyone other than both parents when going to any country not under U.S. jurisdiction.

I learned about this from a very wise travel agent in 1985 when I took my teen-aged niece to Europe. With many travelers booking their own flights via the internet, I find that most people traveling abroad are not aware of this regulation. This information is not readily available on international travel websites, and is often overlooked in guidebooks.

This is the sort of information that can otherwise leave you and your young traveling companion stranded at the airport or pier.

~

My nephew's son, Jake was taking a cruise to the Caribbean islands with his mother (my nephew's ex-wife). She had not been informed of this regulation when booking her trip, despite the fact that she and her son have different last names.

The boy was left sitting in the waiting area in a panic while his mother tracked down my nephew via cell phone so that he could send a fax to the cruise line authorizing her to take Jake out of the country. Had she not been able to reach him on time, they would have literally missed the boat.

~

Before leaving for your Italian adventure, I strongly recommend you **make two copies of documents and credit cards. Leave one copy with someone at home and take the second copy with you, but keep it in a separate place from the original.**

It's also important to leave your itinerary at home, in the hands of a trustworthy person. I never used to do this because when I was on vacation, I didn't want to be tracked down by my boss or co-workers to handle an office "crisis." However, this can cause problems if there is a family emergency, so if you don't want to be bothered while you're traveling, a better tactic is to leave your itinerary with someone whom you trust to contact you only in the case of a true emergency.

I usually put my duplicated documents (passport, credit cards, tickets), along with some extra cash, in a cloth pouch, hidden in my sack of dirty clothes. Never underestimate the power of stinky socks to ward off the potential thief. The originals are stashed in a small, thin fabric envelope, which I keep hidden in an inconspicuous area of my suitcase where a robber would have difficulty finding it.

One other little note of caution--when you're making copies, don't forget to put the original credit cards back in your wallet. I left mine under the cover of my scanner and landed in Italy with only some cash. My sister had to send them to me via "priority mail," which during August in Italy does not exist. I got them almost three weeks later, when I was down to my last 20 euros.

MONEY, CREDIT CARDS & BANKING

What to do about money? Where's the best place to exchange it? What credit cards should you use? Can you use debit cards? This chapter will give you the information, along with a bit more. Some things must be done before leaving, while it is better to do others once you're in Italy. Keep in mind that most of the advice in this chapter is applicable throughout Europe.

It is best to exchange some of your dollars for Euros prior to leaving the U.S., and exchange more after you arrive in Italy. Taxi drivers and hotel bell boys used to accept dollars in lieu of local currency, but with the advent of the euro and decline of the dollar, it is best to assume that whomever you are tipping prefers euros.

The least advantageous places to exchange money or travelers checks are: Italian airports, train stations, and exchange offices. You will get less than favorable rates, and the fees can be as much as twenty percent.

Once upon a time, Italian banks used to exchange foreign currency, but now most only accommodate customers who have accounts there. **So, if you need to exchange currency or travelers' checks, the best place to go is the post office.** You will get the most favorable rate and will only be charged a nominal fee per transaction (in 2013, it was 5 euros). The process, however, can be long and tedious because Italian bureaucrats move slower than flowing olive oil.

It's quicker and easier to use your debit card in the ATM machines *(bancomat)*. The exchange rate is the most accurate, and the fee changes per transaction. You'll have to spend a few more dollars, but if time is at a premium, that's your best bet. If you find a bank or use the post office to exchange money, there are some things you should know. **Places that handle money are highly secured in Italy.**

They are either equipped with a clever system of double doors or have guards at the entrance. To enter most banks or post offices, you will have to pass through two doors. The outside door will either open automatically or at the touch of a button, then quickly close behind you, after which the inside door will open, allowing you to enter the facility. You will need to take a number from a machine located near the entry. In some of the larger post offices, there are two machines that spit out numbers with a choice of transactions listed above it. The transaction you want is "*cambio valute.*" If you're lucky, they may also have "exchange" written in English, and if you are really fortunate, you will find a location that has a special window just for currency exchange.

After you pick a number, you'll have to wait until your number flashes above the windows. This could take five minutes or an hour, depending on the number of customers ahead of you, so be patient....or you can do what I do. If the number I pick is in the hundreds and the number flashing on the screen is in the single digits, I go shopping, get something to drink or go for a walk, then return just in time for my number to flash. **Whether exchanging cash or travelers' checks, make sure you bring your passport.**

Before departure, you must advise the banks that issued your credit and debit cards that you will be using your cards overseas. You should inform them of the dates you will be overseas and the countries you will be visiting. This is especially important if you are planning to be away for an extended period.

~

During one of my trips to Italy, I had taken a charter flight out of Toronto, which required an overnight stay on the return trip. When I arrived at the hotel, the clerk tried to process my credit card, but the card was declined.

"That's impossible," I said. "I only have a couple hundred dollars on it, and my limit is eight thousand."

"I don't know what to tell you," the woman said, looking at me doubtfully. It was clear she thought I was a deadbeat.

Fortunately, I had enough cash left over to pay for the room. Otherwise, I would have been sleeping in a chair at the airport.

When I returned home, I called the credit card company. The woman addressing my complaint told me: "We had to freeze your account. Someone was using your card overseas."

"That person was me."

This exchange would continue to go on like an Abbot and Costello routine, but lacking in humor. Still not absorbing what I was telling her, the woman responded:

"We called your house to verify that you were the user, but there was no response."

"That's because I was in Europe, using my card."

"You should have informed us of this," were her last words.

I didn't understand the logic, since no one ever questions who's using my card in the States, no matter how much or disparate the charges are.

On my next trip, I attempted to call Citizens Bank to tell them when I would be out of the country. This time, I had difficulty reaching the right party. After pushing buttons for what seemed like eternity and not reaching the proper department, in a desperate mood, I tried pushing 0 hoping it would connect me with a live person.

Well, it didn't. It just kicked me back to the main menu. So, feeling even more desperate, I chose the option for "lost or stolen card," and promptly was connected to a customer service rep. I told him what I needed.

"This is not the proper number for that purpose," the young man with a foreign accent, politely told me.

"If you tell me what number I'm supposed to call for that purpose, I will be happy to do so. I've listened to the menu several times and nothing seems to apply," I said, trying to control my frustration.

He searched for several minutes, and then told me, he would "take care of it."

~

After this incident, I wrote to the bank, and advised them of the problem, and I am happy to report that Citizen's Bank has since redesigned their system. The last time I called, I was able to talk to a customer service rep without using a subterfuge. The woman went through proper security protocols, asked where and when I would be going, and then posted a note on my account. It was a relatively simple and painless process: the way a call to a bank should be. Unfortunately, that was not the case with Visa. Despite spending at least twenty minutes on the phone to advise them that I would be using my card overseas, after my first purchase, my card was rejected. When I returned home I had a message from Visa on my answering machine asking me to verify that it was me using my credit card in Italy, followed by a letter advising me they were "freezing" my card because I didn't respond to the phone message. Bottom line: no one "noticed" there was a note on my account stating I would be using my card overseas. So, be sure to carry two credit cards when you travel, and hope that at least one of the providers has the good sense to check your account when the computer flags unusual transactions. .

In an ideal world, you could purchase a prepaid card and circumvent these drawn out procedures. While I have never attempted to use one myself in Europe, some fellow travelers reported having difficulty with them.

Overall, I found that **it's cheaper and more convenient to use ATM cards or charge cards then travelers' checks.** Most establishments only accept American Express travelers' checks and the rates are usually not very favorable, plus the fee can be as high as 20%.

Another problem with travelers' checks is that since many European countries' currency is now the euro, there are few places where money can be exchanged these days, and the ones easily accessible charge exorbitant fees and offer rates that could be as much as 20% lower than the banks.

During my visit to Italy in 2010, I had brought a couple of travelers' checks I had found in a corner of my suitcase. I exchanged them at the train station and the rate was about eight cents lower than other places, plus they charged me a 10% fee to cash them. So, forget travelers' checks. The safety isn't worth the cost.

Use the ATM machine (*bancomat*) and your credit cards. Instructions are in various languages, including English. You don't need to worry about forgetting to retrieve your card because money is not dispensed until you remove the card from the machine. During my last visit in September 2013, I noticed that the exchange I got at the ATM machine was actually better than the rate I received from the post office on the same day. The foreign currency fee from my bank was 3%, the non-Citizen bank ATM fee was $3.00, which is less than I pay at some ATM's in the U.S. It is also less than I was paying during my previous trip in 2010.

Before you leave, you may want to verify what fees your bank charges for overseas transactions and plan accordingly. .

Despite the fees, it is always more advantageous to use plastic rather than travelers' checks, since the exchange rates were the best available on that particular day. When you call your bank to tell them you'll be using the card in Europe, ask them what fees they charge for overseas transactions.

Only take a couple of credit cards with you when traveling. Keep one in your wallet and leave the other in a safe place. This way, if your wallet is lost or stolen, you will only have to notify one credit card company and you will still have a card to use.

One important point: although you can use debit cards to retrieve cash from Italian ATM machines (*bancomat*), you cannot use your debit card to purchase items overseas.

As far as using your debit card in Italian *bancomats*, it is trial and error. I called Citizens' Bank to see what Italian banks would accept my ATM card, but no one seemed to have this information. I also researched on the internet without success. You may have more luck with your bank.

You should not assume that the largest bank will be the one that accepts your ATM card, though. When I attempted to use my bank card at Banca di Roma, one of Italy's major banks, it was rejected. It was the regional Banca dei Fruili that ultimately accepted it. I was also able to use it at UNIBank, which has branches in most Italian cities. The only time you may run into a problem is if you have a debit card issued by a small U.S. bank or a credit union. Visa and Mastercard are accepted at most hotels and other establishments in Europe, although surprisingly, some places may not take American Express. I asked a shop keeper why and she told me they were slow payers.

Some of the smaller restaurants and shops may not accept credit cards of any type, since most Italians don't use plastic as often as we do.

HEALTH CARE & TRAVEL INSURANCE

Check the current copy of your health insurance before departure to verify whether it covers you while overseas. I have Freedom Blue through my former employer, which in the past did not cover me while I was overseas; however, last year the rules have changed and now it does. Next year, it may not. **Medicare does not cover senior citizens outside the United States, but the Medigap plan with foreign travel benefits will.**

If you're involved in an accident or have a heart attack, you will get emergency care regardless of your insurance status. I didn't have to pay when I pulled a ligament in my leg during one of my visits to Italy. I thought it was because I have dual citizenship and, supposedly, am entitled to free emergency health care when I'm in any country that is part of the European Union. However, an acquaintance of mine fell and sprained her ankle in Rome and was also treated free of charge.

I thought it must be Italy's good will policy towards tourists, or maybe it was because the government realizes that with all the narrow, cobble-stoned streets and slick, marbled church floors, someone is bound to get hurt. I later learned that in Italy, visitors are entitled to treatment for situations that are a threat to life or limb. The extent of treatment you get may vary from city to city, so it might help to have extra coverage. Policies change there just like they do in the U.S. so don't assume you will receive free emergency treatment. Check with your closest Italian consulate to get up-to-date information.

Even if you have to pay for your treatment, though, the cost will probably be much less than what you'd have to pay at home. **Make sure to get a copy of the invoice, and have someone translate it into English before you turn it in to your insurance company.**

If you decide to get additional health insurance or trip-interruption insurance, read the fine print to verify exactly what is covers.

For minor ailments such as the flu, stomach viruses or negligible infections, you can usually get treatment from a pharmacist.

~

On a business trip to Milan, my coworker, Bob, had all the symptoms of the flu.

"Do you think you could go down to the drugstore and get me something?" he asked me after a meeting with our customer.

I explained the situation to the pharmacist, who gave me two large pills and told me to tell my colleague to take one immediately and one before going to bed.

That night, Bob called around 7:00 p.m.

He sounded rather dopey when he said: "I'm sorry. I won't be able to meet you for dinner. I'm too groggy."

The next morning, Bob came bouncing down to breakfast. He looked well-rested and peppy.

"I don't know what they gave you, but it was magic. Last night, it knocked me on my ass. I couldn't even hold my head up, but this morning, I feel great."

I was familiar with that type of reaction. My mother used to have a friend who was a pharmacist and she always returned from her trips to Italy with a bag full of amazing over-the-counter remedies.

In Italy, drugstores and pharmacies are not inter-

changeable. If you need medication, you must go to a *farmacia* (pharmacy) and not a *drogheria* (drug store). Each city in Italy is required to have at least one pharmacy open all night. You can find the list and hours of operation in the daily newspaper under the heading of **Farmacia**, which will be marked by one or two crosses (+), and will show the hours of operation *(ore d'operazione)* or hours open *(ore d'apertura)*. The hours are listed in military time (14:00=2 p.m.).

Keep any prescriptions you bring from home in originally-labeled containers, put them in your carry-on luggage and bring a copy of the prescriptions with you. This is especially important if you are diabetic or have any other ailment which requires that you carry needles. In the early seventies, during the height of the drug years, I was severely anemic and had to give myself B-12 shots. My syringes created quite a stir going through customs. I was glad I had secured a note from my doctor.

You actually don't need to bring any more than what you will need during your travels, since you can purchase syringes at a pharmacy without a prescription. Some drug stores even have automatic dispensers located outside the door where pharmacy supplies (medications, syringes, etc.) are available.

PACKING

Travel light. The airlines are charging increasingly more for excessive luggage and heavy suitcases. The limit is usually 50 pounds on U.S. airlines and 24 kilos, which is approximately 44 pounds, on foreign airlines. There are also restrictions on the size and number of pieces of carry-on items. You should contact your airline or research online the weight and size restrictions before departure. If you're traveling by train, you will be responsible for transporting your suitcases throughout your trip.

What and How to Pack

What you need will depend on the time of the year and the locations you will be visiting. Unless you're under twenty-five, **I advise against wearing white athletic tennis shoes and any items with local team names. I would also recommend not wearing shorts in the city.** These items will instantly label you as a tourist, and make you a magnet for peddlers, pick-pockets and gypsies.

The Vatican and even some of the other churches require that a woman's upper torso and arms be covered. They also do not permit shorts or mini-skirts. I have watched tourists stand in line and then not be allowed to enter a church due to improper attire.

If you're planning to visit a casino, bring dress clothes. Some casinos have relaxed their rules and now permit women to wear slacks, but most still require that men wear jackets. In the nineties, I had dinner at a casino in San Remo where the majority of patrons were dressed as if attending a black-tie affair.

Some upscale restaurants also have a dress code that does not permit jeans, shorts, or tennis shoes. I would recommend that women bring at least one pair of dressy slacks, a skirt or dress, and a pair of comfortable dress shoes. Men should pack a pair of dress pants and a shirt.

On the more casual side of things, try to pack clothes that coordinate with each other, don't wrinkle easily and don't require much maintenance. Man-made fabrics such as polyester travel well, but can be horribly warm in the summer. It's important to bring a sweater or light-weight jacket, and comfortable walking shoes. If the shoes are new, test them at home to make sure you are able to walk long distances comfortably.

Most men (and a few women) don't bother with pajamas when they travel. The risk in doing this is that if there is a fire, you'll have to run to the lobby in your underwear (at best), so I always bring pajamas but not a bulky bathrobe.

There is one item that I found to be particularly necessary: a hooded, waterproof jacket (even in the summer). I recommend a jacket rather than a long raincoat, because coats tend to get tangled and can trip you getting on and off of public transportation. For men, a waterproof jacket and a cap (without logo) serve the purpose. Wind can be a problem, so umbrellas often turn inside out. I have a habit of losing umbrellas, so I bring a cheap one from home and if it's still in my possession at the end of the trip, I leave it behind for someone.

As for underwear, you probably have your own idea of how much underwear you are comfortable bringing on a trip. I limit mine to the amount of laundry I'm willing to do. Some people only bring two or three pairs and wash them every night, which means on occasion they have to waste time drying them with the hairdryer, or travel wearing damp underwear. Some people I know carry old ones and toss them out as they go along. One female acquaintance does the same thing with T-shirts so she will have space in her suitcase for new purchases.

You should also be aware that **washcloths are impossible to find in Italy**. If you use one, you must bring your own (even if staying in a hotel). As soon as I return from vacation, I put a couple of fresh ones in my suitcase, so I don't forget to pack them on my next trip.

There is no need to bring extra toiletries, however, as most brand names (including make-up) can be found in most major Italian cities. Unfortunately, they are often more expensive.

You can bring tobacco products and alcohol for personal use. Check the Italian Customs website for the latest regulations.

I have to admit that despite my travel experience, I don't always pack the right clothes. There were a couple of Easter trips to Italy when it snowed in early April and I had to borrow sweaters from my relatives.

If you're headed for the mountains in the spring,

bring boots because there may still be snow in some areas.

~

I remember an incident when I wanted to eat lunch in a scenic restaurant on top of a hill. I was waiting for the cable car, when I was approached by a young Italian man. "Signora, your shoes. No! No! No!" *he said, pointing to my feet and shaking his head.* "Che c'e che non va con le mie scarpe? (What's wrong with my shoes?)" *I asked.* "Non potete andare lassu con quelle scarpette. (You can't go up there in those little shoes," he said, referring to my flats. "C'e neve (There is snow)."

"I'm not going skiing; I'm only going to the restaurant," I said.

"Si, ma dovete caminare su quasi mezzo metro di neve per arrivarci, Vi occorono li stivali (Yes, but you have to walk through a foot of snow to get to it. You need boots.)"

I had to forgo dining in the restaurant with the great view.

~

How to partition your clothes among your suitcases and pack them are two important matters.

If you are traveling with your family, it is better to pack several small suitcases than one large one. This is advisable not only because of the airlines' restrictions, but because it is also easier to store small suitcases on trains and busses, and maneuver them in tiny hotel elevators.

Whether traveling with a family member, friend, or significant other, it is wise to pack half of your stuff in your travel partner's suitcase and vice versa, so if one piece of luggage is lost, you will both have something to wear.

Packing those suitcases to keep wrinkles to a minimum takes patience and practice. Depending on the style of suitcase, I either pack them in a roll, or fold them neatly in three sections. To roll them, I stack several of the same items on top of each other, with the most-wrinkle proof on top, then roll them up and put the rolls side by side in the suitcase. There are several brands of sprays intended to remove wrinkles, but work well only on natural fabrics such as silk and cotton. There is a down side, though. The sprays leave a mild but annoying odor, which could be an issue for people with allergies.

To keep my shoes from getting smashed, I stuff them with underwear and socks.

Travel experts advise you not to lock your suitcase, in case the TSA decides to inspect it. However I always keep mine locked, both en route and in my hotel room. In 2011, on my return trip from Prague, was the first time I have ever had my locks broken by the TSA. One lost lock after more than twenty overseas trips beats the risk of having items pilfered in transit or in my hotel room. The decision is up to you.

Finally, I suggest that you pack a change of underwear, a clean T-shirt, and a pair of socks in your carry-on bag in case your luggage is lost or the flight is cancelled. This is worth doing on your departure as well as your return trip. I came to this conclusion after a night of being cold and wet because of a September storm, spent unexpectedly in a chilly Newark hotel room.

Besides your money and documents, there are several other items you should never pack in your checked luggage: cameras, cell phone and related chargers, jewelry, and prescription medicines. Those should always be in your possession.

What to Wear When Traveling

There was once a time when people got dressed up to travel. I remember the first time I traveled overseas, when I wore a business suit, complete with pumps, stockings and girdle from Pittsburgh to Trieste. I can still feel the pain of spending seven hours on a plane, my stomach constricted by that instrument of torture that was the girdle, only to spend several more hours on a crowded train in high heels.

These days, I've seen travelers wear just about anything—including pants that looked like pajamas. So, now I wear jeans or other comfortable pants, a cotton top, a jacket or cotton sweater, and sandals or easy to slip-off flats, whether I am traveling by plane or train.

When choosing your travel attire, be aware that travel experts recommend that you avoid any polyester-type clothing while flying because if there is a fire, you'll quickly become a human torch.

ELECTRONICS, PHONES & OTHER EQUIPMENT

If you're bringing any type of electronic device that will need to be charged or inserted into the wall, you will need to also bring a converter plug that fits into the outlet. In Italy, the plugs are round instead of flat. Before you leave, **you should ensure that any electronics you bring are compatible with Italian voltage, and if the gadget has two settings, remember to switch the setting before you plug it in. If it is not compatible, you'll need to also bring an adapter.** These items have to be purchased in the U.S. and can be found anywhere luggage is sold.

~

When I was in Sorrento with my friend Janice, there wasn't a hairdryer in the bathroom of the hotel where we were staying, so she used the one she had brought with her. She attached the converter, and then plugged in the dryer. Within ten seconds, the lights went out and there was a smell of burned rubber permeating the air.

Her dryer was not compatible with the voltage. This destroyed the dryer, blew a fuse, and caused the hotel to go dark. Needless to say, the management was not very happy with us, and neither were the rest of the hotel guests.

~

Since the voltage in Italy varies from 115 to 220, it would be wise to check with management before using American electronics in a hotel. Most chargers for cell phones and cameras are designed for various voltages, and can be used with just the converter plug. The same usually applies to electric razors, but not always curling irons.

Not all plugs in a hotel room can be used for charging batteries. If it appears your charger is not working, contact the hotel desk.

If you're still using a camera that requires film, do not store your used or virgin film in your suitcase because if the luggage is scanned, your pictures will be ruined. This problem is only supposed to occur with film of 400 ASA or higher, but don't believe it. The pictures of my trip to Greece and Turkey, which were on 200 ASA film, were ruined because I stored the film in my suitcase. This is not an issue with digital equipment, of course

Most providers will program your telephone so you can use it overseas; however, many people I know who have attempted to use personal cell phones have run into some sporadic difficulties regardless of the type of phone or provider. The situation continues to improve, but there are still some problematic areas. **The only way to guarantee that you can communicate via phone anytime you want requires a satellite phone. Inexpensive, prepaid phones do not work anywhere outside of the United States.**

You will need an adapter with round plugs for any phone's charger.

Since I spend a lot of time in Italy, I have a phone that I use when I'm there and replenish it as needed. When it tells me I'm about to run out of euros, I take it to the good old tobacco shop or newsstand and get it refilled. The only problem is that if I don't use it and replenish it at least once a year, I lose any balance left and the next time I'm in Italy, I have to go to the phone store to have the phone reprogrammed, and that means I'll get a new number assigned.

I attempted to get it replenished when I was in Germany last year but, although I could use it there, I was not able to add money to it because their system is different.

To use a public phone in Italy, you will need a card which is also purchased at a tobacco shop and

comes in various denominations. You cannot use them for overseas calls, though, and they are only valid for a limited amount of time.

To call the U.S. from a public telephone, you will need an international phone card, which can also be purchased at tobacco shops or newsstands. I've never used one, but I understand the rates are reasonable.

The most costly way to call home is to use the telephone in your hotel room. The fees are exorbitant; a few calls home can end up costing you more than the room.

Although calling from the U.S. to Italy can be cheap if you have the right provider and package, calling from Italy to the States is expensive regardless of what telephone you use. A five-minute call to my sister depleted almost 20 euros from my Italian phone.

Most hotels have internet access and computers in their public areas so communicating via e-mail and accessing your social networks should not be difficult even if you don't have an iPad or a smartphone with you. You will also find cyber cafes in most cities.

Some of the train stations have started providing internet access, and it's often available in other public areas, but getting an actual connection can be difficult and time consuming.

The newer trains also have internet capability and the seating is designed so that it is easier for the passengers to use computers.

One other important item you should carry while traveling is a small alarm clock. Hotel alarms and wake-up calls are not always reliable, so if you don't want to miss your train or plane, having your own alarm is a plus.

The clock also comes in handy when traveling by train or bus. If you tend to fall asleep on public transportation, like I do, you can set your alarm to go off a few minutes before the estimated arrival time so you won't risk missing your stop and end up in Venice when you wanted to get off in Florence.

GETTING THERE

Since I began my travels, several gateways have been created to make international travel, if not exactly easier or more efficient, at least more diverse.

What route you will take depends on where you live, how much you want to pay, how many stops you're willing to make, and your final destination.

If you're planning to drive to the airport before departure, be aware that nearby hotels often have special deals where you can leave your car there for up to two weeks for a nominal fee, if you spend the night at the hotel. This is usually much cheaper than parking at the airport for a couple of weeks, and could be advantageous if you have an early flight.

Whether you book your flight through a travel agent, directly with the airline or on the internet, it is important to consider your departure and arrival cities.

Italy has three major Italian International Airports where direct flights from the United States land:

**Milan - Malpensa, Malpensa 2000
Rome - Leonardo da Vinci (Fiumicino),
Ciampino (charters)
Venice (Mestre) - Marco Polo**

For travel to other Italian cities, passengers will have to connect through Rome, Milan or some other European city.

The original Malpensa airport is located about thirty miles northwest of the city of Milan, and Malpensa 2000 is a couple of miles north of that. That's where many transatlantic flights land.

If you're arriving from some other European cities, though, you may end up at the airport of Linate, since it handles domestic and short haul international flights, but no transatlantic.

There is an express train that takes passengers

from the Malpensa airports to the Cadorna station, in the center of Milan. The train runs every 30 minutes during the day and every hour from 9 p.m. to midnight and costs the equivalent of about $15.00. **Alitalia passengers travel for free.** There are also buses that take passengers from Malpensa to the main station (Stazione Centrale), and cost under $12, and from Linate to Piazza Babila or Stazione Centrale.

The most important thing when flying out of Milan is to verify from which airport you are departing. An acquaintance of mine flew into Malpensa, and because it is an international airport, assumed she was flying out the same way, but since she was going via Amsterdam and spending the night there, she was ticketed out of Linate. She didn't realize it until she glanced at her itinerary en route to the wrong airport.

Rome's Leonardo da Vinci, (affectionately known as Fiumicino), is about nineteen miles from the city center and can be reached by train in thirty minutes. A train station is located right in the airport; just follow the signs marked "*Treni.*" The train will take you directly to Rome's main station: Stazione Termini for around $12.00. The shuttle runs from 7:30 a.m. to 10 p.m.

Taxis charge a flat rate to and from Fiumicino to the city center. In 2010 it was 45 euros (about $60). The airport, although large, is very well organized and directions are clearly marked in various languages.

The other airport in Rome, Ciampino, serves domestic flights, charters and some low cost European carriers. Connecting flights to other cities go through Fiumicino; however, if you're staying a few days in Rome, and then flying to another city, you may end up departing from Ciampino, especially if you're booked on the popular low cost carrier, RynnAir.

Venice's Marco Polo airport is located in Mestre, about thirty miles from Venice proper. If you have lots of cash, you can hop the *motoscafo* (shuttle boat) that takes you into Piazza San Marco. The fare is about $100. **You can save**

money by taking the shuttle bus that runs to Piazzale Roma, near the train station, and costs less than $12 and then for another $8 to $12 take the *vaporetto* (bus boat) to your hotel. The bus, which is run by Azienda Trasporti Veneto Orientale, takes about half hour and runs every thirty minutes from around 9:00 a.m. to 11:30 p.m. **An even cheaper option is the buses operated by ACTV.**

Some airports are friendlier than others. **If you happen to live on the East Coast or one of the other cities that have direct flights into Italy, you're fortunate.** Since I live in Pittsburgh, the most stressful part of my journey is making the connections.

If you're booking online, the routing choices are limited by the site you're using. Booking through a travel agent, or directly with the airlines may give you a few more options. You can design your own itinerary and book each leg of the flight individually; however, besides costing more, it means you will be responsible for retrieving and rechecking your suitcase(s) at each destination. So, unless you're traveling with just a carry-on, it is not something I would recommend, even if you're willing to pay the extra cost. I tried it once, and it wasn't a pleasant experience.

My favorite route, so far, is Philadelphia to Venice. The international terminal in Philadelphia is within walking distance from most domestic terminals; the Venice airport is small, and transportation into the city is cheap. I believe USAir is the only airline presently covering that route, and the price is not always the cheapest.

If you live in the Midwest, Detroit is a good choice. The airport is compact and easy to maneuver, and since you don't have to leave the secure area to get to your connecting flight, you won't have the pleasure of being fondled by the TSA staff for a second time.

The Logan airport in Boston is usually quite efficient, despite the fact that you have to take a van to get from the international to the domestic terminals.

New York's JFK Airport is large, crowded and chaotic; I try to avoid it if at all possible, but since it's the largest east coast connecting airport, this is sometime difficult. If you're routed through there, you will need time and patience.

Flying through Newark wasn't an unpleasant experience, except for the fact that my return flight to Pittsburgh was delayed and then cancelled due to a storm, which happens often with the smaller planes used by most airlines that service the east. This is especially true during hurricane season.

Some of my fellow travelers like the Washington D.C. airport, but I have no personal experience with that route.

The information provided above is the latest available at this time.

Regardless of what airport you choose, make sure you schedule connecting flights at least one hour apart (more if possible) so that if your domestic flight is late, you won't miss the connections. This is especially true for airports where the domestic and international terminals are far apart. Below is an example of what happened when I disregarded this rule.

~

My friend Angie had made reservations for us through a small travel agency and didn't realize the personnel were inexperienced in international travel. The agent had booked our connecting flights only a half an hour apart. When we looked at our tickets on the day before departure, we almost had a stroke.

"Oh Crap!" I screamed. "We'll never make it in time. If our flight is late getting to Boston, we're screwed."

Our flight arrived on time, but Logan airport was under construction, so the shuttle that moved passengers from terminal to terminal took an excessively long time.

After what seemed like hours of bumpy riding, Angie and I looked at our watches. Our flight was due to leave in mere minutes. Like we were in a bad version of "I Love Lucy," we jumped off the bus and started to run around the construction, outpacing the shuttle we'd just abandoned.

We arrived at the gate just as the doors were closing and got the worst seats on the plane. This was before the scrutiny that resulted from 9/11. In today's security climate, we would not have made it.

~

There is one shortcoming that seems to be pretty consistent in U.S. international airports--a lack of bilingual workers (except for a few who speak Spanish). This can result in confusion and delays as bewildered foreign passengers wander around, trying to figure out where they should go.

~

I disembarked in Newark with a plane full of Italians, few of whom spoke English, and these are some of the comments I heard:
"*In quale fila andiamo? (In which line should we go?)*"...
"*Dove si va a prendere le valige? (Where do we go to get our suitcases?)*"

A burly security guard, who may be best described as a "large, handsome woman" addressed the group in a husky voice, trying to direct the arriving passengers where to go.

"U.S. citizen to the left... Foreigners to the right..."

The Italians stood there, bewildered and confused. Their brows furrowed, as they attempted to catch what the intimidating woman was saying.

She waved her massive hands to show people where to go, telling them: "No, not there...line four...keep moving...don't stand there blocking traffic...move...move!"

She screamed louder and louder, shoving them in the right direction. I felt sorry for my fellow passengers. It brought back memories of when I first came to America as a bewildered child who didn't understand a word of English.

"These people don't speak English. Talking louder isn't going to make them understand. They're not deaf," I said to the big woman.

She shrugged her shoulders and gave me a look that said: "That's not my problem."

I stood next to her and translated her directions into Italian until everyone was in the proper line. She walked away without even thanking me. "Tell your boss he'll be receiving my bill," I yelled after her with a laugh. "He needs to hire some bilingual people." I was serious about that.

~

If you're flying or connecting on Alitalia or any of its partners, make sure you check the monitor for gate changes. The airline changes gates regularly and often the new gate is on the opposite end of the airport from the original one. They usually announce the change, but sometimes the announcement is only in Italian and they seldom repeat it. I almost missed my flight from Rome to Trieste because I was in the bathroom when the announcement was made.

As for which airline to choose, I have flown on most of them and see little discernible difference in the comfort or service when flying in the coach section. What stands out in my mind is that the food is often better on foreign than domestic carriers. If time permits, I usually eat before boarding the overseas flight en route to Italy, drink a glass of wine and am asleep by the time dinner is served. This way, I can get a couple of hours of sleep before people start parading to the bathroom and avoid consuming the in-flight meal.

As a rule, the best time to fly is mid-week (Tuesday, Wednesday, or Thursday). That's when flights and airports are the least crowded and it's easy to find more price bargains. You can now pick your airline seat via the internet or your travel agent prior to boarding, and some airlines offer a choice of the "premium" seats which allow a little more leg room, for an extra fee.

If you're a frequent flyer with that particular airline and arrive at the airport early, you may be able to get upgraded to those seats for free, if they are still available. Regardless, there is no great comfort when you fly coach overseas.

I have to admit that air travel during the last few years has not been as much fun as it was the first few times I flew to Europe. One of today's many unpleasant aspects is going through security. The TSA has become progressively more aggressive.

Two years ago, I flew back from Europe via Amsterdam and besides a body scan, I was also given a very personal pat-down. I wondered what would have happened if, like some of my friends who have had mastectomies, I had been wearing a prosthesis.

I asked a young man I know who works for the TSA why the security guard felt a pat-down was necessary after a full body scan, and he said it's usually done if you're wearing a belt, jewelry or have something in your pocket. I had none of the above, except for a very visible watch around my wrist. My thinner friend, who was wearing a belt and several pieces of jewelry, didn't get patted so I question the rule.

I think the security system needs to be overhauled with some sensitivity and common sense applied, but until this happens, be prepared to be exposed and manhandled, and get to the airport in plenty of time.

TRAVELING WITH YOUNG CHILDREN OR PETS

Depending on the number of children and their ages, it may be easier to rent a car if traveling with young children, since it's difficult to travel light when you have to carry diaper bags, bottles and sip cups.

Few public bathrooms in Italy have diaper-changing facilities, and not all hotels have cribs; therefore, verify that they will be able to meet your child's needs before you book. The same applies to high chairs or booster seats in restaurants. They will do their best to accommodate you; just give the restaurants a call in advance so they can prepare. Diapers (*panolini*) and other baby supplies can be purchased at a *drogheria* (drug store) and usually in the children's section of department stores. **When buying diapers in a drug store, make sure you don't get confused: *panolini* are diapers; *panolini igenici* are sanitary napkins; *pannoloni* are incontinence diapers.**

Restaurants don't offer children's menus because European children eat what their parents eat, but you can order half-portions (*mezza porzione*.). Children are allowed in bars as long as they are accompanied by an adult.

Animals are permitted on most airlines; however,

they may end up with the luggage. If your pet weighs less than 10 pounds and the carrier fits under your seat, some airlines will let you bring it on board, but you may have to pay extra. Rules change regularly and vary with each airline, so check before you book.

Your pet will not have to be quarantined as long as you have the proper papers showing it has been vaccinated, and you're flying from the U.S. directly into Italy. If you stop in some other country, that may not be the case. The U.K. is especially strict and if you land there, you will have to quarantine your pet.

Many hotels allow dogs. You can take small dogs on public transportation and the outdoor areas of restaurants, as long as they are restrained. You can also bring them into many stores, except some establishments selling food.

Places where dogs are not permitted sometimes have steel hoops or bars outside their door where you can tie up your animal before you enter. I've passed butcher shops, and grocery stores where several dogs were parked outside while their owners shopped. The amazing thing is that I've never witnessed a dog fight; they all seemed to get along peacefully. Service dogs, of course, are permitted anywhere.

I have seen cats in carriers on public transportation, but as far as hotels are concerned, check before you book.

Italy is a pet-friendly country; however, I have to admit that Italians don't do as good a job cleaning up after their dogs, especially in the parks and other green spaces, so beware.

Small pets in carriers are permitted on trains. Larger dogs can travel on most trains if they are muzzled and on a leash. You may have to pay a fee on certain trains if traveling during peak hours. You will need documentation certifying your pet has the proper vaccinations. Check the Trenitalia website for the latest guidelines.

ONCE YOU HAVE ARRIVED

ACCOMMODATIONS

Where you stay depends on your finances, means of transportation, and individual expectations. Since I lean towards the less expensive and spend little time in my hotel room, I usually prefer small, economic, European hotels. I find them more charming and intimate than American chains, or sprawling, fancy hotels. I also feel safer there since they are unlikely to be infiltrated by intruders or be targeted by terrorists.

TYPES OF ACCOMMODATIONS

There are various types of accommodations available in Italy: the traditional hotels (*albergo*), bed-and-breakfasts (*pensione*), villas, furnished apartments, hostels and-nonconventional places, such as convents, monasteries and farm houses (*agriturismo*). In some cities, you can also find day hotels (*albergo diurno*) where travelers can shower and change. I have stayed in most of these; below are details on those worthy of elaboration.

Bed and Breakfast

A B&B (*Pensione*) in Italy could be a small, quaint hotel, or a room in someone's home with a shared bathroom. They can be charming and comfortable or minimalistic. They are an inexpensive option if you're on a tight budget or want a more homey feeling than a hotel. In some of the smaller towns, *pensioni* are the only options. If you are fussy about accommodations, I would recommended you either get input from previous guests or see the place in person. Most *pensioni* provide breakfast; others will not. Some may also provide other meals. Usually, there are not public spaces available except for a breakfast room. Some do not accept credit cards or reservations far in advance.

Villas

The name "villa" can be deceiving. When we think of villa, we conjure up visions of a large estate in the country. A villa in Italy could be a rustic farmhouse in the Tuscan countryside, a converted castle on a hill, an opulent residence by a lake, a cottage by the sea or just a free-standing home in the suburbs of Milan. (My Italian relatives refer to my modest home as a *viletta*.) Villas are the most expensive type of accommodation, but if you are planning to stay in one area and traveling with family or a group of friends, a villa may be the best way to go. They are usually located outside the city center, so you may need a car to get around. In some cases, a cook or a housekeeper is provided. The internet is a good source for villa rentals. Before you commit, though, make sure you are getting what is advertised. I would strongly recommend you request a reference from a previous tenant, when guest comments are not available online.

Apartments

Apartments are a good option if you're planning to stay a week or longer. The biggest advantage of renting an apartment is that you can do your own cooking and laundry. This not only saves the expense of eating out, but also provides you with a better opportunity to mingle with the locals and absorb the culture. The price of apartments varies greatly depending on the amenities, location and length of stay. You will pay as much to spend a week in a modest apartment in Venice as you would to stay a month in a fancier place in a non-touristy city. In a college town, there will be more apartments available at lower rates in the summer when school is not in session.

If you're traveling in the winter, ask about the heating situation. In some apartment buildings, the heat is automatically turned off during the night. You should also inquire if linens are provided or if you need to supply your own. The most important thing to remember when looking for an apartment is to ask questions and specify your requirements.

Don't assume anything.

~

The first time I rented an apartment was in 1998. I was going to be spending a week in Trieste after touring other cities, and since my mother was also there visiting relatives and planned to remain for the entire month of June, I decided it would be nice to rent a two-bedroom apartment. I didn't have the time or tools to do research, so we asked my cousin Arianna and her husband to find a suitable place for us. We wanted something with a private bathroom, in the city, close to public transportation.

Several weeks prior to departure, my mother called me at work. I could hear the excitement in her voice, "Piero found us a nice place. It's less than 2 million lire. Is it okay?"

Two million lire equaled less than a thousand dollars, which I thought was reasonable for the monthly rental of a two bedroom apartment. After years of traveling, I was suspicious of something that sounded so good.

"Where is it located? We don't have to share a bathroom, do we?" I asked, anticipating some potential issues.

"It's near the main hospital, in a high-rise off Via Ginnastica."

I was satisfied with this. I knew the area was conveniently located near the city center.

My mother went on, "It doesn't have a bathtub, but Piero said there's a large, modern bathroom with shower and laundry. It's on the top floor, so we won't have anyone stomping around above us."

I really wasn't too concerned about overhead noise, but my mother obviously was.

"It sounds OK... I'm assuming there's an elevator. I don't cherish lugging our suitcases up several flights of stairs."

"Oh! I'm sure there is one. Piero knows I'm seventy-eight-years old," my mother said confidently.

I believed her. After all, who would put an elderly woman and her fifty-something daughter on the top floor of a high-rise building without an elevator?

Our young relative Piero, it turns out.

There was no elevator! Being active people in the prime of their lives, our relatives didn't consider the fact that older people may have difficulty climbing several flights of stairs on a daily basis.

The spacious apartment was located in what Italians call an edificio d'epoca—a historic building. We had to lug our suitcases and groceries up 232 marble steps.

Luckily, it was situated near several good, inexpensive restaurants, so we didn't do much cooking. We left in the morning and tried not to return until evening. As we huffed and puffed up those marble steps, I reminded myself that the hospital was conveniently near-by. This turned out to be a blessing when my mother twisted her ankle on those steps, the week after I left.

There was one bright spot, though...all that exercise permitted me to consume a large number of those tasty Viennese pastries for which Trieste is famous.

~

If you're renting an apartment, there are a few other things of which you should be aware: gas stoves in Italian apartments have a conveniently located safety switch that completely turns off the gas after cooking. This also applies to the water in the washer. This prevents gas or water from escaping in case of a malfunction or pipe corrosion.

Italians have been conditioned to conserve energy long before the propaganda to go green. Some hotels and apartments have hall lights that come on when you exit the elevator or walk by the monitor, then automatically turn off after a few minutes. Apartments also have separate hot water tanks in the bathroom and kitchen that can be easily turned-off when not in use. In many cities, the heat in apartment buildings is automatically turned off during the warm weather (usually from April 1 until October 1).

Hostels, Convents and Monasteries

Hostels were once designed mainly for students under twenty-six years old, but now are patronized by older travelers as well, including senior citizens. They consist of a dorm room with multiple beds, and a shared bathroom. They are the cheapest type of accommodation and a good way for people with limited income to see the country. They are available in major cities and college towns.

Although I have never stayed in a convent or monastery, people who have admit that the rooms are comfortable as well as inexpensive; it can also be an interesting experience. However, it is worth considering that these places may have early curfew times or other restrictions.

Farm Houses (*Agriturismo*)

Some farmers have opened up their homes and rent rooms or complete farmhouses to tourists who want a more rural experience. Many homes are equipped with swimming pools and provide bike rental. Most also accept pets. You can find information under *agriturismo* on the internet.

Day Hotel (*Albergo Diurno*)

An *albergo diurno* is a place where a traveler can shower, change and freshen up. They are usually located in or near airports, or close to public transportation. If you are arriving from an overnight flight, a long train ride, or spending part of a day (but not overnight) in a city, you can rent these facilities for a period of time. Most consist of a room with a shower, toilet and sink; others resemble a gym's locker room. *Alberghi Diurni* are functional but not fancy.

DEFINING REQUIREMENTS

My travel commandment is: assume nothing. Don't assume that your "private bathroom" will have a shower, toilet and sink. If you require a bathtub, inquire if one is available. Do not assume that the room you book, the one listed as "having multiple windows," will actually have a view. Above all, don't assume that your relatives, friends, or fellow travelers who are recommending places to stay have the same prerequisites you do.

When booking a room, don't assume that the

amenities to which you are accustomed at home will automatically be available. This is true for large hotels as well as the smaller inns. **Temperature can be surprisingly important.** Most Italian hotels installed some form of cooling system after the heat wave of 2003, but Americans who are used to staying in places where you need flannel pajamas at night may not find the Italian version of air conditioning adequate. I prefer fresh air and usually travel off-season, so I've never suffered from excessive heat, but I have been cold on a couple of occasions.

Not long ago, I spent an April night when the temperature dipped into the forties, freezing my fanny in a lovely Florence hotel. Apparently, after April 1, the heating system automatically shuts off. I'm not sure if it was the hotel policy or a government regulation to save energy. **So, if being warm in April or cool in August is important to you, check before you book.**

Elevators present another issue. I have encountered some charming hotels in Venice that did not have elevators. The bell boys will carry your luggage, but if you have difficulty walking up a flight or two of stairs, it wouldn't be the place for you to be. Not all hotels have facilities for the handicapped; however, most will go out of their way to accommodate them.

I suggest that you clearly define the requirements which you feel will ensure the enjoyment of your trip. My requirements are very basic: a clean, comfortable room with a functional bathroom. Proximity to the city center or public transportation is also important to me.

Addresses can be deceiving. Verify on a map that you can actually access the places where you wish to go. My friend Aggie stayed at a nice, reasonably-priced hotel not far from the Vatican in Rome, but it was located on a main highway that she had to cross to get anywhere.

You may not be able to get all the amenities you want for the price you are willing to pay, so I recommend you choose the three or four things that are most important to you as a traveler. Below are some additional factors that you may wish to consider before booking your accommodations:

- How are heating/cooling handled for my room?
- Is there an elevator? How far is my room from it?
- How often are rooms cleaned? Bedding changed?
- Proximity to areas that interest you.
- Is the area easy to navigate on foot?
- Room size
- Double bed vs. single beds

In my early days of travel when I had little disposable cash, I used Arthur Frommer's book *Europe on $5 a Day*, and actually stayed in places that cost less than $5. (Of course, this was back in the early seventies, when you could book a room at the Holiday Inn in suburban Chicago for $6.00 a night.) The rooms were sparsely furnished and the bathroom, which I shared with several other guests, was located somewhere down the hall.

I still use Frommer's guide, but now pick from the higher categories instead of the least expensive ones. I also use various other sources to select my accommodations: travel magazines, fellow travelers and the Internet. One of the best Internet sites for booking accommodations (including apartments) is **www.venere.com**. This site is easy to navigate, provides ample information and good value for the room prices.

When using the Internet to select accommodations, read the reviews and comment section of the page. Be sure to take into consideration the age and nationality of the writer. What's acceptable to people who may be used to living in confined quarters, without air-conditioning, may not be satisfactory for Americans. On the other hand, things that an older guest may find inconvenient may be perfectly suitable to a younger person.

~

During one of my trips to Italy, I stayed at a small hotel in Vicenza (Hotel Continental). The place wasn't fancy, but the bed was comfortable, the breakfast was plentiful and it even provided heated towels in the bathroom, as well as a pitcher of refreshing punch as you entered the lobby in the evening—all this for only 55 euros (about $75) per night. Yet, there was an elderly couple from New York who gave the hotel a bad rating. The main reason was that it was located about a mile from the center of town.

~

If you're the adventurous type of traveler, and you wait until you arrive to book a room through the local tourist office, keep in mind that they may not always direct you to the hotel with the best value. They will pick from the hotels that have listed with them—hotels that may not be listed elsewhere, including the Internet.

HOTEL STARS & SINGLE ROOMS

European hotels are rated with stars, but the number of stars doesn't always correspond to the quality of the accommodations. Hotels located near the train or bus stations are usually rated lower and cost less than the ones near the major tourist sites. Places in city centers may be noisy regardless of price or stars. A three-star hotel in Lucca may be better than a four-star hotel in Rome. Also, some hotels purposely keep their rating low to avoid higher taxes.

In the popular cities, you'll get less for your money, but you can still find some bargains. In Rome, I found a nice little hotel, halfway between the train station and the Coliseum for only $110 per night. I would have paid twice as much for the same accommodations closer to the monuments. Had I gone in August instead of September, I could have stayed at the same place for 25 percent less because Europeans escape to the sea or the mountains in August.

Most Italian hotels have single rooms to accommodate lone guests. The price is usually twenty to thirty percent cheaper than that of a double room. Some hotels also offer the option of single occupancy rates for a double room. That rate is slightly lower than the double rate. **The biggest disadvantage of single rooms can be the location.** They are either tucked in a corner next to the kitchen, the elevator, or some other undesirable spot.

I always book a single room when traveling solo, and have had a mixed bag of experiences. I stayed in a room in Milan that was so small I had to close the bathroom door to get into bed, and one in Florence where the only window faced the back alley where the garbage was kept. In San Remo, though, I landed in a small, but beautiful single room that had a balcony with a view of the beach and was furnished with antiques, and on a visit to Lake Come, I had a spacious single room overlooking the lake.

The actual location, amenities, and price of your room depend on the hotel you choose, the time of year, and how early you arrive. This often applies to double rooms as well.

~

On my last trip to Rome, I reached the hotel in late afternoon, so I was assigned the last available single room. It was quite comfortable with weathered but attractive furnishings and a large, ceramic-tiled bath. Unfortunately, it was situated next to the rather noisy elevator, and the window faced the equally loud air-conditioning unit. I actually had to stuff my ears with toilet paper to get a good night's sleep.

~

Many hotels in resort areas require that you take at least "half-pension"---which means eating at least one other meal besides breakfast at their facility. A few require that you eat all your meals there.

Italian law requires that room prices be posted in each hotel room, and a receipt be issued upon payment. You should keep the receipt until you leave the country. Most hotels, even the ones that don't accept credit cards,

will require either a card number or deposit when booking.

CHECKING IN

Don't be embarrassed to ask to see your room before registering; most European travelers do this. When you **check into any hotel, the clerk will take your passport and hold it for a few hours or overnight.** The reason for this **is that all people visiting Italy must make their presence known to Italian authorities within eight days of arriving.** The clerks of wherever you are staying usually fill out the necessary form, which is why your passport is required.

In Italy **the bottom floor is referred as the ground floor (*piano terra*) rather than as the first floor.** The floor numbers start with the second floor, so if the desk clerk tells you that you're in room 103 on the first floor, it's not on the ground floor, but what we consider the second floor. I know people who have spent hours looking for their room on the wrong floor.

Unless you're staying in an ultra-modern establishment with key-card entrance, **you are required to turn in your key every time you leave the hotel premises and pick it up when you return.** This is a way for the staff to keep track of who's in and out, and schedule housekeeping.

Most keys are either the size of a small wrench or have a heavy ball attached to them, so it's unlikely you'll forget to turn them in unless you have an extremely large purse or deep pockets.

Most small hotels close their doors at night, so if all the keys are gone, the night clerk assumes the guests are inside and locks the door. **Some hotels close their lobby door at a certain time (usually 11 P.M. or midnight) regardless of whether everyone is in or not,** and guests must ring a bell if they return late. If you return after closing time and have not deposited your key at the desk, you may have difficulty being admitted.

I remember standing in the rain outside a hotel in Torino, reciting my address and birth date, so the night clerk could reassure himself that it was really me trying to get in after 11 p.m. and not some intruder. Of course, had I been a thief who had stolen my purse and passport, I would have had all the required information, plus the key to my hotel room. So, it is important to leave the key at the desk.

ITALIAN BATHROOMS

The bathrooms in most U.S. homes and hotels may be different in size or design, but the apparatus is basically the same. It consists of a shower and tub, combined or separate; a toilet in various shapes and colors, and a sink. The operation of the faucets is not usually a mystery. Some public facilities have automatic flush toilets, or faucets that magically operate when you wave your hands in front of them, but even those are basically standard.

This is not the case in Italy or anywhere else in Europe, for that matter. Most Italian bathrooms are a mystery to be discovered, whether in a home, hotel or other public places. First of all, don't assume that "private bathroom" means your hotel room or bed & breakfast will have a complete bathroom as a separate facility similar to the one in your home. You could be in for a surprise.

~

I once stayed in a pensione where the tiny bathroom contained a shower and a sink, but the toilet was down the hall. My strangest experience was a room in a small hotel where the shower was in a closet-like space, and (to my surprise) the toilet and sink were in the sleeping area. This amounted to no privacy. Since it was a single room, they figured I wouldn't need it. However, I did need it because the tall window, which was only covered by sheer curtains, faced the toilet. Anytime I went to the bathroom, I envisioned a stranger staring at me from the building across the street.

These situations are the exceptions because most hotels have the standard private bathrooms, **but if the information you have available isn't specific, verify exactly what "private bathroom" entails.**

The bathroom in a hotel can be the size of your living room or your walk-in closet. I've stayed in an old hotel in Venice where my line-dancing troupe could have practiced in the bathroom, and slept in a place in Pisa where my knees touched the sink when I sat on the toilet.

The bathtub, if there is one, can also vary in size or shape. If the hotel is in a building dating back to the 19th century, you will probably find a tub large enough to drown in. With short legs like mine, getting in and out of those has been a challenge, even in my younger days. In those places, the shower often consists of a showerhead that can be adjusted up or down. In other places, there may be a short, deep tub with a porcelain seat built into it.

Showers can also vary from place to place, but I found most are smaller than the ones in the States, and not designed to accommodate seriously large guests. Some are surrounded by a glass enclosure, while others are just an area in the bathroom with a drain separated by a shower curtain, where the water often ends up all over the floor. Despite the difference, they are usually quite functional.

Figuring out how to operate the plumbing and adjust the temperature can also be a mystery and may require trial and error. Just make sure you place a bath-mat on the floor because the slick, ceramic tile can be quite slippery when wet. I spent two weeks hobbling around with a knee brace because I forgot to take that precaution.

The sinks, whether pedestal or cabinet, are basically the same as in the States, although my tall friends have complained that they are too low. **One important note: the C on the faucet handle does NOT stand for cold. It's for** *caldo***, which means hot in Italian. The cold water faucet is labeled F for** *freddo***.** There is usually a red or blue dot, along with the letters, but guests sometimes miss it. Confusing hot for cold can have serious consequences because the hot water is often scalding. In some public bathrooms, the faucets are operated by foot levers on the floor beneath the sink.

One item that is rarer than gold in Italian hotels' bathrooms, is a wash cloth. I have asked many of my fellow travelers, some of whom have stayed in fancier hotels than I, and no one remembers ever seeing a wash cloth. I don't recall encountering one in any European hotel.

Most of the hotels where I've stayed, whether large or small, have been equipped with a bidet. What is a bidet? It's something that looks like a seat-less toilet with a spout that squirts water up instead of down. The main purpose of the bidet is to wash one's private parts, but I found it useful for other purposes, as well. I'm surprised it hasn't caught on in the U.S. I only know of one person who has one.

~

When I saw a bidet in my hotel room, on my first visit to Italy, I thought: "How nice. There's something where I can wash my clothes." Then I noticed a bidet in the home of one of my relatives, and since they had washers, I figured it must serve some other purpose. It took me several days to muster the courage to ask about it.

"Excuse me Leda, but what is that thing for? I've never seen one before," I asked my relative.

"Really! You mean you don't have them in the U.S.?" she said, shocked. "How do you wash yourself after going to the bathroom or when you have your period?"

That brought up a lengthy discussion involving the quality of our toilet paper versus theirs, but solved the mystery of the bidet.

~

Over the years, I've found numerous uses for the bidet, other than the one for which it was intended. Besides soaking my unmentionables, it's great for quickly washing my feet after walking around the dirty streets of the city.

The toilets can be anything from a large, marble throne to a hole in the ground. Unless you're staying in a very low-budget hotel, the toilet in the room will probably be the standard white porcelain type. The challenge is to figure out how to flush it. None are designed the same way as ours.

Some have a square device built into the tank's top or side, or a foot lever on the floor. If the water tank is located high up near the ceiling, there is usually a dangling chain to pull or a button on the wall to push. Sometimes the button is located on the wall behind the toilet and invisible when the lid is up. There could also be a lever on the ground, besides the toilet. Flushing is baffling to most first time tourists.

I was in the bathroom of a restaurant in Pisa, when I heard someone in the next stall yell: "Does anyone know how to flush this toilet? There's no lever on the tank."

"It's the button on the wall, over the toilet," I replied.

Public bathrooms, especially in restaurants, are often co-ed.

I remember the time my friend Gerry came out of a café bathroom pulling up her pants and screaming: "There's a man in the next stall."

During my Europe 101 course, I had forgotten to warn her about the shared bathrooms.

Some public bathrooms are what I call "semi-co-ed." A main door marked *gabinetto* (toilet) leads into an entry which is usually equipped with a sink. Then there are separate facilities for men *(uomini)* and women *(donne)* on each side of the entry. This can be very confusing. I can't count the number of times I have walked out of the ladies' room, washed my hands, and then wondered into the men's room instead of out the main door. I'm particularly prone to do this in restaurants, after I've had a couple glasses of wine.

Train and bus stations have separate facilities, but you usually must pay a set fee before using them, or there's an attendant by the door who solicits donations.

The locking mechanism in public bathroom is often a challenge. I probably hold the record for the number of bathrooms I've had to break out of in a variety of unusual ways. There were occasions when I've crawled like a snake under the tiny space beneath the door, or stood on the sink to climb over the entrance.

~

I once had to spend two hours in the bathroom of a Venetian restaurant. The door locked with a large wrought-iron key, but when I tried to exit, the key wouldn't work.

I was the last lunch customer, and the restaurant was preparing to close, as most do in the afternoon. I pounded on the door, but no one answered. I could hear the clanking of glasses and dishes and a distant conversation. Finally, I started screaming.

"Aiuto! Sono chiusa nel gabinetto. (Help! I'm locked in the toilet.)" I yelled until I finally heard the sound of footsteps.

I passed the key under the door to see if the manager could open it from the outside, but it didn't work. One of the waiters also tried it without success.

"The lock must be jammed again," the manager announced. "You'll have to wait until we get the locksmith."

(Like I had a choice.) Over an hour later, I was finally free. Since I'm no longer agile enough to climb over or under bathroom doors, I now leave them unlocked if the locking mechanism appears to be the least bit complicated. Better to be exposed than locked up.

~

Men's rooms are equipped with the usual urinals and often don't have doors on the stalls. I guess whoever designed them assumed men didn't need privacy. How do I know about the men's room? I've had to visit them sometime when the ladies' room wasn't operational and, as I have mentioned before, have accidentally wandered into them on occasion.

Toilets in public ladies' bathrooms sometimes lack seats. I don't understand the reason. I assume they are easier to keep clean that way.

The most interesting type of bathroom, though, is what the Italians refer to as a "Turkish bathroom." It is a hole in the ground with two indentations for the feet on each side. It causes shock and dismay, and although it may be adequate for men, presents a challenge to any woman who has to use one, especially if she's wearing slacks.

~

My cousin Lisa told me about her experience during her trip to

Italy, when she was still a teenager.

"*I walked into this bathroom in a restaurant, and all I saw was this hole in the ground with a chain above it. I thought it was a shower. When my parents told me it was the toilet, I didn't know what to do. I was trying to figure out how I could use it without peeing on the bottom of my slacks.*"

"*I rolled up my pants and bent down. I was scared I would slip and fall,*" she said. My challenge these days is not so much peeing on my clothes as being able to squat down and get back up without falling. Fortunately, there are few of those bathrooms left around the country.

~

A type of facility, which is quite popular on the French Riviera but has just recently emerged in Italy, is the automated toilet. In France, they are found on the main drag in the center of towns, especially near beaches. I have only seen one in Italy, and don't recall exactly how it operates. All I remember is that the door opens after you put a coin in the slot, and then quickly closes after you enter. A few minutes later, the toilet flushes and the door reopens. I had my friend stand guard, and would never use one again unless I had someone with me. Given my history with toilets, my biggest fear was that the thing would malfunction, and I'd either be stuck there forever, or the door would open prematurely and I'd find myself sitting on the toilet in the center of town.

As an adult making plans to return to Italy for the first time, I remembered the unique texture of Italian toilet paper—it was like wiping your derriere with a brown paper grocery bag. Therefore, the first time I returned to my native country, I packed a roll of toilet paper. However, the quality has improved tremendously over the last twenty years, and you can even find some of our brands in the supermarkets. So, there is no longer any need to bring paper.

This is not always true for public bathrooms, though, especially the free ones. If there is toilet paper in the stall, it's usually the cheapest and flimsiest available. Also, in some of the bathrooms where there is an attendant on duty, she will hand you one tissue-size piece of paper, after you've deposited your donation. (I'm not sure what happens if you don't drop any money in her basket.) So, it is wise to keep a pack of tissues, or better yet, some baby wipes in your purse or pocket. Some toilet paper manufacturers in the States now make adult flushable wipes that are perfect for this type of situation.

On a side note, I have found Italian bathrooms to be a great source of humorous conversations.

ELEVATORS

Elevators in Italy are as interesting and unique as the bathrooms. Most are much smaller than ours. Some of the ones in hotels and apartments are so small that, if you have several pieces of luggage, you'll have to bring them up one piece at a time. Many of the elevators in older buildings have large, iron grates in front of them that either open automatically or have to be pulled open when the elevator reaches the ground. Others have double doors—an inner, sliding door, and an outer door which has to be opened manually. The inner door will not open, and the elevator will not run when the outer door is open.

It's a safety precaution, so people don't fall down the elevator shaft, but it can be annoying. If you're in the lobby waiting and someone on the fourth floor forgot to close the outer door when exiting, you will be there until a person on that floor takes the elevator or closes the door.

I have taken many hikes to and from hotel lobbies, and even my cousin's fifth-floor apartment, because some inattentive person forgot to close the elevator's outer door.

When riding an elevator, remember that what Americans usually consider the first floor is what Italians consider the ground floor. It will be marked on the buttons as O (zero) or T for *terreno* (ground) or PT for *piano terreno* (ground floor). Hotel lobbies are sometimes located on what Americans would consider the second floor, which in Italy is the first floor (even if you have to

walk up a flight of stairs to get to it). In that case, the elevator's first and next-to-last stops will always be at the lobby, so guests can pick-up and deposit their keys.

HOW TO GET AROUND

Italy has excellent infrastructure, so getting around the country is easy. Most Italians travel via train or car, but sometime flying is cheaper, especially since the emergence of some discount airlines such as Ryanair.

VIA TRAIN – FERROVIE DELLO STATO (ITALIAN RAIL SYSTEM)

The train is my favorite way to get from city to city. It's comfortable, cheap and convenient. You get to see the country and meet interesting people. Also, trains are not at the mercy of traffic. The newer, faster ones have panoramic views and hookups for electronic equipment, but I prefer the older trains with the individual compartments that seat six and can be converted into an actual double bed. I spent several nights on trains during my early days of travel when I couldn't afford to stay in a hotel every night. I have had some interesting experiences and met the most colorful people on those old trains.

~

In the early eighties, while traveling from Vienna to Venice with my friend Gerry who hadn't traveled much, we encountered a young boy who had escaped from what was then communist Poland. He looked to be in his early teens and his only luggage was a small duffle bag. His corduroy pants and flannel shirt appeared well worn and faded, and his ear-length blonde hair had the disheveled look of someone who'd spent the night on the train without the benefit of a comb.

I sensed there was something wrong by the way he was perched at the edge of his seat and kept eyeing the door. Whenever he heard a noise or a compartment door opened, he jumped up and looked out into the hall. I suspected he was traveling without a ticket.

"Ticket man come?" he finally asked in extremely fractured English.

"Yes! But he'll probably come again after we cross the border into Italy," I told him. He was young enough to be my son; I felt sorry for him.

"I guess you don't have a ticket," I said smiling, enunciating every word. "Where are you going?"

"Veneto. See parents."

"Parlate Italiano?" I switched to Italian, hoping it would be better than his English, and it was.

He told me he had escaped from Poland without money or passport, and was going to try to find relatives who lived in a small town in the Veneto region of Italy. I didn't know if his story was true or not, but he appeared too young and scared to be dangerous. I gave him $20, which I figured would cover the ticket price from Venice to his destination, and we shared with him the cheese, bread and fruit we had brought for lunch.

"Unless you're a criminal, the Italian authorities will try to help you," I reassured him. He wasn't convinced. When we approached the border, he hid in the bathroom, and we never saw him again.

Gerry was in shock when I told her he was a fourteen-year old runaway.

Then, en route from Venice to Trieste, we met a not-very-famous Italian movie star whose name I don't recall. He had been in Hollywood trying to make it big, but had just ended up working as a stand-in for Lee Van Cleef in some old "spaghetti westerns." He had given up on the movie business and was returning to Trieste to open a burger joint, which he was convinced would be hugely successful. I didn't want to burst his bubble by telling him I couldn't see the Triestines flocking to a fast-food joint. Four years later when I returned, the restaurant had already closed.

Traveling via train has a few disadvantages. Unless you pay to have it shipped, you're responsible for your luggage from beginning to end, which can be daunting if you're overloaded with stuff. Trains are also crowded in the summer, on weekends, and on holidays.

TYPES OF TRAINS

Eurostar Italia Alta Velocita -- These are high velocity trains that travel between major cities. The *"Frecciarossa"* (Red Arrow) travels at 175 mph; the *"Frecciargento"* (SilverArrow) travels at 125 mph. (They are shown on the timetable as ES, AV or ES-AV.) It's a great way to go if you need to get somewhere fast; however, their speed makes it difficult to enjoy the panorama. These very modern trains are air-conditioned, outfitted with hookups for electronic equipment, and are set up with tables which are ideal for laptop use. They also have separate, modern bathrooms for men and women. They are handicap accessible and have ample storage for luggage. When traveling on these trains, you can have your luggage shipped door to door for as low as 20 euros.

The Frecciarossa has a restaurant car where passengers can enjoy a full meal at reasonable prices. The Frecciarento features a buffet bar.

They connect major cities across Italy.

Frecciabianca (WhiteArrow) – These are slower trains that run often and connect eighty-seven medium and large cities throughout Italy. They do not have a dining car. Some have a "corner bar" where you can have coffee or a drink and socialize; others just have a refreshment cart that travels through the cars, serving sandwiches and drinks.

Intercity Trains: Diretto, Regionale and Locale (Express, Direct Regional and Locale) -- Don't let the labels *espresso* and *diretto* fool you; these are all slow trains. The *espresso*, *diretto* and *regionale* stop at various cities within an area; the locale stops at every little town on its route. Some still have the old-fashioned compartments, which seat six; the *locale* has airline type seats, but with a lot more leg room. Some of the newer cars have double decks. They don't usually provide refreshments; you have to bring your own.

In the older trains, some of co-ed bathrooms leave a lot to be desired, and are often out of order, out of toilet paper or the sink is not functioning. I suspect it's a way of discouraging people from using them unless absolutely necessary. Since the excrement goes directly from the toilet onto the tracks, you are not permitted to use the facilities while the train is parked at the station. I assume some travelers were not abiding by these rules, because lately the bathrooms have been kept locked until the train is on the move. I discovered this when I tried to wash my hands after eating a particularly sticky and tasty pastry while waiting for the train to depart.

These slower trains do not require reservations. Tickets for these voyages can be used on any day for up to two months.

Euronotte - Treno Notte -- These are night trains with various types of accommodations, and are the most comfortable way to travel from one end of the country to the other. Details can be found on the Trenitalia web site.

The majority of these trains are air conditioned. Trenitalia is in the process of upgrading their fleet, so check their website prior to departure for the latest information.

You can find up-to-date information on all these trains on the Trenitalia website.

MAIN STATIONS IN ITALY

Rome - Stazione Termini is within walking distance from all the major sights. The Vatican has its own station, called Roma-San Pietro. Not to be confused, there are two other stations located in suburban Rome: Roma Triburtina and Roma Ostience.

Florence - Firenze Santa Maria Novella (SMN) which is in the city center is the primary station. There's a smaller station outside the city, with frequent trains to SMN.

Venice - Venezia-Santa Lucia is located a short walk from St. Mark's Square and Rialto. In front of the station, you can also catch the *vaporetti* (boats) that transport passengers along the Grand Canal. **The Venezia-Mestre** station is located about fifteen minutes from Santa Lucia, in the industrial suburb where the airport is located. There are trains that run every half hour or so between the two stations.

Milan - Milano Centrale is a mega station located in the center of the city, close to the *Duomo* and the *Galleria*. It's one of the main interchanges of Europe. Trains from the airport arrive in Milan Cordona, a small station also in the city center. There are three other suburban stations: Lambrate, Porto Garibaldi and Milano Rogoredo, the last of which is quite a distance from the city.

Turin has two main stations in the city center. Torino Porta Nuova, which is the larger terminal and Torino Porta Susa.

From the above listed major stations you can get to the rest of the train stations in Italy.

TICKETS, PASSES & RESERVATIONS

Second-class tickets are about 35% cheaper than first-class tickets. The seats in the first class railcar are more plush, but not worth the extra cash unless you're traveling during peak travel times, or over long distances. Many of the *regionale* and *locale* trains do not have a first class car. Second-class can be crowded during the summer and on Fridays and Mondays, especially if you're traveling anywhere near a university town.

~

Three years ago, I was on a Friday afternoon train from Venice to Senigallia, and as we passed through Bologna, the compartment filled with students going home for the weekend. There were not enough seats, so they sat on their luggage in the aisle and carried on competing conversations with their cell phones until they reached their destination. It was not a relaxing experience, plus I had to crawl over some of them when I disembarked. I was wishing I had bought a first class ticket.

~

Under the present guidelines, I would not recommend using the Eurail Country Pass (Trenitalia pass). Once upon a time, you could purchase a country pass that would allow you to travel for two, three, or four weeks for a flat rate. It permitted passengers to get on and off the train as often as they wanted, and the only extra fee was for reservations, which were usually not mandatory. This is no longer the case. The country passes now available only allow the holder to travel for three to ten days over a two or three-month period.

This year (2013), the cost for three days of travel is $247 in second-class. Considering the fact that you will have to pay a premium of 10 to 15 euros plus the cost of reservations on certain trains, and will have to wait in line to get them, I don't see any advantage in purchasing a pass.

If you do decide to get any type of pass, be sure to have your passport with you on the train because you will be required to show it, and follow the instructions for pass validation. **All passes have to be purchased in the U.S.**

I found it is much better to visit the customer service desk in the train station, tell the clerk the stops you want to make and when you want to go, and he will print you individual tickets with the necessary reservations. This will save you time and money. Do this as soon as you arrive, because there is often an advance purchase discount on certain routes. Three years ago, I traveled from Trieste to Venice, Venice to Senigallia, and Senigallia to Rome for 39 euros (about $50). A Eurail pass that allows three days of travel would have cost $205, plus the price of reservations.

Individual tickets are quite cheap, and there are often discounts and special bargains available. The Trenitalia website will provide up-to-date information, since prices and special deals change regularly.

This year (2013), besides the flexible **Base** ticket that can be changed as often as you like up to an hour after the train departs, Trenitalia is offering two types of discount tickets.

An Economy *ticket where you can change the time* and date once until departure. There is also a **Super Economy** starting at 9 euros on the Frecce Trains. These tickets are non-refundable and cannot be changed. The number of seats available at these lower prices is limited and varies from train to train.

Trenitalia only accepts certain credit cards, and the site is not always easy to navigate.

Any tickets can be purchased in the U.S. via a travel agent or on the Eurail or Trenitalia website; however, they could cost considerably more than buying them at the station in Italy. This year, my ticket from Venice to Monfalcone cost me 9.4 euros (about $12). Had I bought it in the States prior to departure, it would have cost me 15.7 euros (about $20).

You can purchase tickets at the station from the ticket machines on the day of travel or in advance. The instructions are in various languages (the button with the U.K. flag will access the English version). Some machines only accept credit cards, and the ones who accept cash can only dispense a limited amount of change. If you insert a 20 euro bill and your ticket only costs 9 euros, you may get a an I.O.U. slip for the change that you will have to redeem at the customer service counter.

This can be a time-waster. Also, sometimes the machines are out of order, which can be annoying and time-consuming if you have to run from machine to machine to find one that's functional. If you're buying multiple tickets for various connections, I recommend you skip the machines and get your tickets from a real live person.

Tickets for short distance trains do not require reservations and can be used for up to two months. Long-distance, fast trains require reservations. There are usually seats available even for same day travel, except for around holidays.

Sometimes, if you're brave enough to travel during certain Italian holidays like May 1 (Labor Day) or August 15

(Ferragosto), the Italian railway offers dirt cheap rates on certain trains. Plan to get to the station early, fight your way onto the train, and be jammed in with a herd of colorful individuals, some of whom have no sense of common courtesy.

You can get some cheap fares, but you may have to suffer some discomfort. Regardless of how much you pay for your ticket, traveling around holidays can be a painful experience. Besides tourists, there are the students returning home from school.

Trenitalia sells more tickets than there are seats, and even if you have a reserved seat, you have to fight your way past people sitting on their suitcases in the aisles.

On two occasions I have had the misfortune of traveling on Good Friday, and would never do it again.

You can find up-to-date details on trains and discounts on the Trenitalia website. Just keep in mind that the prices quoted are more expensive than what you will find at the train stations in Italy.

VALIDATING TICKETS

Certain tickets for the slower trains require validation before boarding. This prevents the traveler from re-using the ticket. **The third line on top of the ticket will state "*da convalidare*,"** and there are several small machines located on the platform by the tracks for that purpose. (They used to be bright yellow, but some of the newer ones are green or blue.) The ticket should be inserted in the slot of the machine. If you forget to do this, you will have to pay a fine, which is at least the equivalent of the value of the ticket, on the spot.

I have to admit that I have been guilty of neglecting to do this on a few occasions. The controller let me slide a couple of times, due to extenuating circumstances--after lecturing me on the importance of validating. On one occasion, though, I had to pay the fine.

Ignorance of the regulations or not understand-

ing the language is not usually an acceptable excuse. I had to explain this to a group of Canadian students who were getting fined during a train ride from Florence to Verona.

BOARDING THE RIGHT TRAIN AND RAILCAR

This is an area where travelers can sometime get into trouble. I once encountered a group of tourists who ended up in Florence from Venice, instead of the Italian lakes where they had wanted to go. I got into a little trouble myself, on my first trip back to Italy.

~

I was taking a train from Milan to Trieste, and checked the schedule board that showed there was a train leaving at 10 a.m. I bought a ticket and hopped onto the car that happened to stop in front of me when the train pulled into the station. A couple of hours into the trip, there was an announcement, in both Italian and English, which stated that cars six and seven were going to be disengaged at the next stop and attached to a train headed towards Rome.

I had no idea what railcar I had hopped, but after asking some fellow passengers where they were headed, realized that I was on the wrong one. I grabbed my luggage in a panic, and fought my way through several cars in the moving train until I found a railcar that was headed east towards Trieste.

~

So, to ensure that you don't land somewhere you don't want to be, you need to do three things: get a map of Italy, check the placard on each railcar, and learn the Italian name for the cities. The reason for the latter is that although train stops are usually announced in both Italian and English, the name of the cities is in Italian (i.e. Venice = Venezia; Florence = Firenze; Rome = Roma).

The placard, which is located on the side of each car, lists the names of all the cities where that particular car is headed. If you're on a train that does not require reservations, you can hop on any car headed to your destination.

If you have reservations, however, you will need to find the specific car and seat assigned to you. Your ticket or reservation slip will list your railcar and seat number.

In many train stations, there is a chart near the platform that shows the composition of each train. This will help you determine approximately where each railcar will stop. You can position yourself on the spot in front of where the car number listed on your reservation will land, and hop right on.

Finding your seat is not very complicated. Each railcar has a number printed on the side. Once you enter, you can locate your seat (just like on a plane). The number is listed somewhere above the seat. On the older trains, the seats that are reserved will have a tag in a pocket above them, which states *"riservato,"* or there may be a placard on the door of the compartment that shows which seats are reserved. If you end up sitting in a seat reserved for someone else, the seat's "owner" can and will oust you. I know because it's happened to me on a couple of occasions.

All of the above sounds very complicated, but it really isn't. My niece Lisa, who was sixteen when I took her to Europe, figured out the routine by the third train ride.

To simplify the above process, here are some easy steps:

1. Determine what time you want to depart. Check the train schedule that is posted in each station. It will indicate the time of departure, track number, type of train, all the stops and times of arrival at each stop.

2. Purchase a ticket. If a reservation for the chosen train is required, the ticket will include it and will state on top: *Biglietto con Prenatozione* (Reserved Ticket). If it needs validation, the ticket will just state: *Biglietto* (ticket), the type of train, then the statement *Da convalidare* (To be validated).

If a change of trains is required to get to your fi-

nal destination, you will get two tickets--one from your city of departure to the city of transfer, and one from city of transfer to your final destination. If you are using the machine, wait for both tickets to pop out.

    3. Just before departure, validate the ticket (if required) on the yellow machines at the platform. (If in doubt, just validate.)

    4. Check the overhead display in the station to confirm from which track your train is departing. (Sometime, it changes from the one listed on the schedule board.)

    5. Check the chart on the platform to review the composition of your train, if necessary. When the train is approaching, move to the approximate spot in front of where your car will be.

    6. Board the train, and if you have a reservation, look for your seat.

LUGGAGE HANDLING

On the *Freccie Rosse* and *Freccie Argento*, you can have your luggage delivered door to door for a fee. Otherwise, you have to handle your own bags. You can carry as much luggage on board as you wish without paying a fee, but you're responsible for it from beginning to end. Depending on the type of train and size of luggage, it can be stored on the overhead shelf, behind the seat, or on a rack at the end of each wagon. Although I've never lost a piece of luggage, I admit that I'm a bit anxious about leaving my suitcase at the end of the car, so I try to get a seat where I can see it.

Something to keep in mind when determining how much luggage to take, and a good incentive to travel light, is the fact that in certain towns you have to use an underpass to exit the station or to get to the track from which your train is departing. This means dragging your suitcase up and down a flight of stairs, since the majority of these stations don't have elevators.

~

During one of my early trips to Europe, I bought a large denim suitcase which I filled to the brim. At that time, suitcases didn't have wheels. I was leaving directly from work, so my brother picked up the suitcase, stopped in town to get me, and then we headed for the airport. I didn't know I was in trouble until I got to the check-in counter and realized I could barely lift it. I found porters at the Milan airport, but this was not the case at the train station, so I had to drag it on the ground to the train. Being young then, I was able to find some helpful men who lifted onto the wagon.

I stopped in the small town of Cuneo, in northern Italy. I had planned to check my suitcase, meet a friend for lunch, then catch the train to Rome. To get from where I had gotten off the train to the luggage storage room, I had to pull the suitcase down a ramp of about twenty steps and then back up another one. It was a small station, so there were no young men to come to my aid. After lunch, I didn't have the energy to haul the suitcase up and down the twenty steps to the departure track again, so I broke the law--I crossed the tracks. This is not something I would recommend.

I wasn't in serious danger, since I had checked the schedule to make sure there wasn't a train due within the next few minutes.

I was barely across the tracks when I spotted the railroad police charging after me. They appeared annoyed and angry. I was not exactly thrilled, either. I was thinking about the hefty fine I would have to pay for crossing the tracks, which equated to an entire week's worth of my salary at the time.

"Signora! Signora!" They yelled as they chased me across the tracks. I prayed that they didn't speak English.

"Non si puo' attraversare il binario. (you can't cross the tracks)," they said, pointing at the clearly visible signs that were written in Italian and French (but fortunately, not in English).

I shrugged my shoulders and acted bewildered. "Sorry, I don't understand Italian," I lied.

They gestured and pointed, waving their arms, as I shook my head, pretending not to understand a word.

After several minutes of yelling in Italian and French, not to mention numerous hand gestures, some of which were not polite, they finally walked away, shaking their heads and muttering: "Mamma Mia! Cosa dobbiamo fare con questi stupidi di Americani? (What are we to do with these stupid Americans?)"

I figured it was better for them to think I was stupid, than to have to pay such a high fine. I felt guilty for deceiving them, but paying the penalty would have depleted quite a chunk of my cash, and have caused me to cut my trip short.

Just as the train departed, I watched the policemen talking to the baggage clerk, who knew I spoke perfect Italian. They started to chase the train, screaming what I felt sure were obscenities at me, but I was gone. I smiled as they made some hand gestures in my direction. I'm not a law breaker, so I wasn't proud of my behavior. It was the first and only time I have ever done anything so risky.

Instead of heading for Rome, I took a detour to Trieste, dropped off my enormous bag, and borrowed my grandmother's beat-up, twenty-four inch leather suitcase which I used for the rest of the vacation.

~

That experience taught me to pack lightly. Now, I've learned to travel for several weeks with just a twenty-two inch suitcase.

If you're just planning to spend the day in a city, you can store your suitcase at the station for a nominal fee. Most stations either have a manned storage facility or lockers where your suitcase can be placed. Fees vary by location, but prices are usually reasonable.

STATION FACILITIES

Amenities vary from station to station, depending on the size and location, but all have two basic services--a bathroom and a newsstand. As far as food is concerned, most Italian train stations, to my great disappointment, are now serviced by McDonalds. I'm not a Mickie D's fan, but I walked into several of their establishments to see what was on the menu. It was pretty much standard fare. The buns appear different though, and they do provide ice with their soda, which is unusual in Italy, but you can't get your soda or coffee to go. Some also serve beer and wine. The stations not serviced by the Golden Arches have a coffee shop or snack bar where you can purchase sandwiches, candy, cookies, soda and other quick snacks. Since Italian coffee can be consumed in one gulp, coffee for takeout is impossible to find. At the small stations where there isn't a restaurant or coffee shop, you can usually purchase water, soda or snacks at the newsstand.

The style and cleanliness of train station bathrooms differ greatly from station to station, but if you plan to use the bathroom, you better carry some coins because few are free. Since I resent having to pay to pee, this is one custom of my native country of which I am not proud. In some cases, there's an attendant who either charges you a fee, or asks for a donation; in others, there are automatic doors that only open after the required coin is inserted, or there's a slot on the stall door for the change. This fee is supposed to ensure that the facilities are properly maintained. (More information on bathrooms can be found in the "Italian Bathrooms" section.)

~

I'd love to get my hands on the man who designed the bathroom in the Venice train station. It's the only facility available to meet the needs of the hordes of tourists who arrive every few minutes, so there is always a long line of people waiting to use it. The last time I was there, I ended up having "words" with the attendant.

To get to the stalls, you must insert a two-euro coin (almost $3) into a slot which causes the glass front doors to magically pop open. Since you can only use a two-euro coin, there is a machine on the wall that changes paper currency into coins. The problem is that travelers aren't aware of the amount required until they reach the front of the line, which slows down traffic while they get change.

On that particular day, the change machine was out of order and the attendant was nowhere in sight. So, there were people waiving euro bills in the air, screaming: "Do you have 2 euros?" "Avez-vous 2

euros?"…"Avete 2 euro?"…"Haben Sie 2 euro?" Everyone needed change.
 I came prepared with a two-euro coin in hand, and then helped a few people who needed coins. Finally, I got to do what I needed to do. When I came out, a couple of French women who weren't able to get change were tying up the line, while people behind them were yelling and cursing in various languages. So I held the glass doors open and let the ladies pass through without paying.
 At that precise moment, the attendant returned from wherever he had been and started screaming at me. I tried to explain to him about the broken change machine, but he wouldn't listen and continued berating me. I won't repeat what I replied, especially since it would lose its flavor in the translation. All I can say is that he must not have been a Venetian boy, because he looked puzzled when I called him a jerk in the local dialect.
 I have to admit, though, that despite the masses that pass through that bathroom, the place was clean and well maintained. On my visit in 2013, I noticed they had reduced the price to only one euro.

~

 I discovered an easy way to avoid the bathroom hassle. I stepped out of the station, turned left and walked into the ice cream parlor which is located next door. I sat at a table, ordered two scoops of ice cream that cost 2.5 euros, and used their bathroom. The only setback was that I had to walk two flights of stairs to get to it. Table service, which is slightly more expensive than just buying an ice cream cone, is required to be able to use the facilities.

TRAIN SAFETY

 I have traveled alone on a number of Italian trains over the past forty years without any safety issues. However, my incident-free travels can be attributed to more than a long streak of good luck. I have developed a number of techniques that have assured the safety of my possessions on the train, and I encourage you to do the same.

If you are like me, the consistent swaying motion of the train may tend to make you drowsy, which is not the ideal state for watching your belongings. Because of this, I always try to sit by the window so that I can place my well-fastened purse between my body and the compartment wall. If this isn't possible, I place it securely on my lap with my arm through the strap.

Traveling at night requires even more serious monitoring of your possessions. While most of my travel has been done during the day, in the few instances when I have traveled at night, I discovered that the best way to watch my purse is to sleep on it. Use it as pillow or neck rest, or cradle it against your body like a baby. This applies even if you're in a sleeping car or have the compartment to yourself.

As for cameras and other electronics, don't store them in your suitcase. Keep them with you in your carry-on, and construct a mini-trap, perfect for any petty thief preying on tourists. Store the bag beneath your legs, and place the strap or handle around your ankle. This way, anyone wanting to steal your photos of the Sistine Chapel will have to fight you to get to them. I have done this many times, and have returned home with the same amount of valuables I brought on board.

Men also need to be careful with their wallets and other valuables. They should keep them in a pants pocket that isn't easily accessible. My brother had an unpleasant experience during his train travel.

~

Late one night, Dan was taking a train from Florence to Venice and was peacefully asleep, lulled by the rocking motion of the railcar. He woke up to discover his pocket watch was missing. It was a special watch that he had purchased at an antique sale, which was equipped with an alarm.

My brother scanned the area for suspects, and spotted only one-- the young man who had been sharing the compartment with him. Dan questioned the man.

"Did anyone come in here? My pocket watch is gone," my

brother asked.

The man crossed his arms and stiffened.

"I don't know anything. I was sleeping," he answered in a defensive tone.

"You're sure you don't know anything?" my brother said calmly. He used his authoritative "school teacher" tone that allowed the suspect the benefit of a doubt, and gave him the opportunity to confess.

"No. I don't know," the young man insisted as he shifted uncomfortably in his seat.

"OK!"

My brother was fairly sure the man was lying, but didn't pursue the issue. He calmly looked out the window and smiled.

He was still smiling a few minutes later when he left the compartment.

"I'm going to the bathroom. Keep an eye on my stuff," he said to the suspect, who didn't catch the sarcasm.

Dan found the conductor and, in his best Italian, said to him: "I'm pretty sure the kid sharing the compartment with me stole my pocket watch. In another fifteen minutes, just before we arrive in Venice, the alarm should go off. I would appreciate it if you would be outside the door when it does." He then described the watch in great detail to the man.

Dan returned to the compartment still smiling. Sure enough, at the prescribed time, a persistent beep emanated from the young man's pocket. He jumped up, startled, and attempted to leave, but was stopped by the conductor who had been standing outside the compartment door.

"Signor, fatemi vedere cosa avete nella tasca. (Mister, let me see what's in your pocket,)" the conductor asked, in a polite but firm tone.

The young man tried to claim the watch was his, but had a hard time explaining how Dan knew exactly what it looked like and at what time the alarm would go off.

When the train arrived in Venice, the thief was turned over to the "polizia" and the watch was safely back in Dan's pocket.

~
MISCELLANEOUS TRAIN INFORMATION

Don't be surprised if you see a dog or cat in a carrier

or bag on the train. Italy is quite pet friendly and Trenitalia allows the transport of small dogs and cats. The rules vary depending on the type of train, but the animal must always be restrained.

You can also take your bicycle on the train. The guidelines for storage depend on the type of train. The Trenitalia website or information desk at the station can advise you.

TRAIN STRIKES

When train employees decide to strike, it's usually sudden. The strikes are called "*sciopero a singhiozzo*" (hiccup strikes). The work stoppages are of short duration, a few hours or a couple of days, but if you're planning to travel at that particular time it can cause havoc on your plans. However, bus companies often increase service and replace train routes during train strikes. Occasionally, all public transportation goes on a sudden strike. If you're unlucky enough to be caught in such a situation, then you are in serious trouble. Fortunately, this does not happen very often.

TRAVELING INTERCITY VIA BUS

I have only traveled via bus when visiting small towns not serviced or easily accessible by train. Bus fares are relatively inexpensive. Going via bus has some advantages and disadvantages: you are at the mercy of traffic and busses are more confining than trains. If traveling long distances, the views are usually monotonous, since buses travel on major highways. The biggest advantage is that your luggage is usually stored underneath, and you don't have to carry it onto the vehicle.

Most Italian cities have regular bus service to nearby towns and some of the other major cities, especially those not easily accessed by train. Bus stations are often located near the train station. You can get schedules and information on bus service from the local tourist office, or even your hotel. Tickets can be bought from a clerk or machine at the station, or sometimes even on the bus. There's usually a machine to validate the ticket, by either inserting it in a slot or scanning it, as you enter the bus. In some cases, the driver will take it, partially rip it, and return it to you.

DRIVING

Despite having spent many months in Italy, I have never driven there. One of the reasons is that I'm intimidated by the crazy drivers. Also, it does not make financial sense for one or two travelers to rent a car, since public transportation is cheap and readily available, while car rental and gasoline are expensive. **There are also additional insurance expenses incurred when driving in Italy.** The main advantage of renting a car is that it enables you to easily reach remote destinations, and you don't have to drag your luggage onto public transportation. If you're traveling with young children, driving may be the best option.

The highways (*autostrade*) of Italy are in excellent condition and the signs are clearly marked in various languages. The *strade statali*, which are secondary roads, are not as well-maintained as the major highways, and roads in certain regions of Italy (mostly in the south) may not be up-to-par. **In the cities, street names are difficult to read when driving because they are located on the sides of buildings, and the streets are narrow and hard to navigate. Drivers also need to contend with the menace of scooters weaving in and out around cars on city streets.**

Most Americans I know rent a car at the airport, drive through the countryside or into small towns, but will not venture into the center of the larger cities. It takes real courage and a touch of masochism to do so. Besides the aggressive drivers, narrow streets, and erratic traffic patterns, there is the issue of parking which is usually at a premium, confusing, and extremely difficult.

Italians have their own way to solve the parking problem. I once watched four men in Florence as they took a little Fiat, lifted it off the ground, and placed it in a parking spot where it could barely fit. The funniest sight, though, was during my first trip to Italy in the early seventies. I spotted an American trying to maneuver his large Cadillac convertible through the narrow streets of the little town of Muggia. After scraping his fins against a building a few times, he parked it at the edge of town and traveled on foot.

~

If you decide to rent a car and drive, you should be aware of the following:

Don't assume anything. If you want a car with automatic transmission, air conditioning or other amenities that are taken for granted in the U.S., specify your needs when making reservations. Italian cars are small, so if you're traveling with several people and a lot of luggage, you will probably need a car with a luggage rack or a mini-van (another good incentive to travel light).

There is an extra charge for picking up the car at an airport or train station. Also, beware of extra taxes and fees when getting a quote.

Make sure your credit card covers car rental in Italy. Some do not. Most rental rates in Europe include liability insurance, which does not cover damage to the vehicle itself.

Some companies include collision damage waiver (CDW), which is not always included in the rate but is required in Italy, so you may need to purchase it separately. You will also need to purchase theft-protection insurance. Make sure you verify exactly what your insurance covers. Friends of mine recently had a minor accident, which the rental company said wasn't covered by insurance, and it cost them $800.

Americans who have driven in Italy also recommend that you rent in the States from an established American company so that if there are any disputes, you can resolve them when you return.

Gasoline stations in the city follow shop hours and, except for those on the main highways, may not be open on Sundays and holidays. Some are self-service; others still have attendants. The speed limit on highways is usually 110 km per hour (about 70 mph), and about 50 kmph (30 mph) around the city. Payment of tolls is required to drive on the superhighways (*autostrade*). The tolls can be paid in cash, credit card or via prepaid cards that can be purchased at the tobacco shops.

Seat belts are required, and children must be restrained, although the rules for child car seats appear to be less stringent than ours. Check with the car rental for up-to-date details.

Headlights must be turned on while driving on major highways, even in the daytime. Drivers take the rules seriously, and law enforcement considers any infringement a primary offense. **There are also serious repercussions for driving under the influence.**

Getting around any major Italian city by car presents a challenge for even the most experienced driver; however, there is one city where I strongly discourage tourists from ever driving—Naples. Drivers weave in and out of traffic without signaling, and consider lights and stop signs a mere suggestion. Unless you have a death wish, stick to public transportation; take a bus or cab, hold on tight, close your eyes, and pray.

CHAUFFERED CAR

If money is not an issue, the most stress-free and luxurious way to tour Italy is to hire a chauffeured limousine or car. You can find information online or at the tourist desk of any Italian airport. It's a convenient way to travel, but may deprive you of potential adventure and cultural experiences. I have never tried it, but it's an option I may have to consider when I'm too old to travel via public transportation.

If you are planning to venture on any of the nar-

row mountain roads like the ones around the Amalfi coast, I would recommend hiring a car with driver or a taxi. Those roads are difficult to maneuver; one wrong move could send you careening down a ravine. A group of us hired a cab to go from Naples to Pompeii and then to Sorrento. The cost was minimal when split four ways, and the driver even serenaded us as he drove.

GETTING AROUND THE CITY

BUSES & STREETCARS

Modern Italian cities have cheap and convenient bus service. **Tickets for the buses can be purchased at tobacco shops (*tabaccheria* marked with a T) or magazine stands,** where you can also buy weekly or monthly passes as well as bus schedules.

In some cities, there are also machines that dispense bus tickets. Just make sure the machine reads **"Biglietti Autobus."** When I was in Amsterdam, where I don't speak the language, it took me three tries before I actually got bus tickets. The first time, I got stamps; the second time, I got condoms. Both are useful items, but not to ride the bus.

Most buses have separate entrance and exit doors; individual tickets must be validated by machines located near the entrance doors. Monthly or weekly passes are dated, and validated with a date stamp the first time they are used. In most cities, people travel on the honor system. The bus driver does not monitor whether tickets are validated or passes are legitimate; however, periodically there's an inspector who boards the bus and checks passengers to ensure they have a validated ticket or a pass. If a passenger is caught without a valid ticket or holding an expired pass, he is required to pay a steep fine on the spot.

The inspector is dressed in plain clothes with only a badge to identify him, and meanders through the bus. Some inspectors check the ticket of every passenger; others check only the ones they deem suspicious. During all my years of travel, I have spotted the inspector only a few times. On one of those occasions, I watched a young man who was without a valid ticket being hauled off the bus.

Purchasing and validating tickets is an area that can be confusing to first-time visitors. It certainly was to my brother.

~

After his first trip to Italy, my brother commented: "Isn't it nice that you can ride the bus for free in Trieste."

"What do you mean for free? You have to buy tickets."

"I took the bus to Michela's house, and I didn't see anyone depositing any money or buying a ticket so I assumed it was free."

"Didn't you see people punch their tickets on the machine by the door?"

"I watched and didn't see anyone doing anything. They just walked in and sat down."

"They probably had passes. You're lucky you didn't get caught, or you would have had to fork out a couple hundred bucks on the spot."

Since most people in Trieste use passes, he didn't see anyone validating tickets and assumed transportation was free.

After validation, bus tickets may be good for just one ride, forty-five minutes, one hour, or ninety minutes, depending on the city.

At bus stops, there are signs indicating the letter and/or number of the busses that stop there and sometime there is also a schedule posted. In some cities, there are maps that show the bus route posted at the primary downtown stops. **Buses only stop on request and are hailed like we hail taxis in the U.S.** When their bus is approaching, passengers step off the sidewalk and wave their right arm.

Bus drivers in Italy have a tendency to speed through the city like Mario Andretti at the race track, so you better hold on tight or you may end up on the floor. Busses are crowded even during non-peak periods. **To get off, you have to stand by the exit door and push a button that signals a request to stop**...and move fast.

The front seats are reserved for elderly and hand-

icapped passengers. If you are sitting in one and an older or disabled person enters, you are required to give up your seat. If you do not, the bus driver can force you to do so, although I've seldom seen that happen. I realized I was showing my age when young people started offering me their seats (which I never accepted as a matter of pride, no matter how tired I was).

Small pets are usually permitted on buses as long as they are contained. In some rural cities, you may also find people carrying small, caged farm animals. You're allowed to transport luggage; however, if you are carrying a large suitcase and the bus is crowded, the bus driver may not let you on, or force you to exit.

In cities popular with tourists, you can usually get a tourist day-pass that allows you to get on and off a bus to see the sights. You can inquire at a tourist information desk or at the customer service counter in the train or bus station.

A few cities still have the old-fashioned streetcars that operate basically the same way as the buses, and Rome has special busses that operate all night. These stops are marked with an owl sign. Tickets for those busses can be bought on board.

Note: The public transportation company of Milan is called Agenda Transporti Milanesi (ATM), so in Milan when you see an ATM sign, it designates public transportation and not an ATM (bank) machine.

TAXIS

Taxi stands can be found at bus and train stations, near hotels and other strategic spots throughout the city; however, the best way to ensure that one will show up is to call from your hotel or restaurant, or to arrange for one in advance. Attempting to hail a taxi will seldom get you results.

Make sure you board an official Taxi and not a jitney (it should have a Taxi sign on top). You will be

charged extra for each piece of luggage (another reason to travel light). In some cities, there is also an extra charge at night and during Sundays and holidays, and there are established fees for trips to and from the airport. If there is no set fee, you can negotiate a fare prior to boarding.

Taxis charge an initial flat fee and then a per kilometer rate. The meter starts ticking the minute the taxi leaves the stand. It's wise to get a map, figure out the approximate mileage to your destination and pretend you know where you're going, even if you don't. Most taxi drivers are honest and will drive the most expeditious route to your destination, but there are a few who will try to take you for a scenic tour instead of going directly where you want to go. Some will actually point out sights as they take the longest possible way to your location.

Before you complain, though, make sure there is not a legitimate reason for the routing change, such as construction or other restrictions. During a visit to Vicenza, I noticed that the taxi driver veered from the route my map indicated. I was getting ready to protest, when I realized my hotel was on a one-way street and the driver had to go around the block to get to the entrance.

If you're in a city such as Milan, Rome and especially Naples, and happen to take a taxi during peak traffic times, fasten your seat-belt tightly, close your eyes, grit your teeth, and pray. Drivers will weave in and out of traffic while yelling, cursing and gesturing. One of my friends who suffers from motion sickness usually takes medication before boarding a taxi in Rome.

As for tipping, tip your taxi driver what you would normally give to a taxi driver in the States.

SUBWAYS & FUNICULARS

Rome and Milan have subways (*Metropolitana*) that are convenient and very easy to navigate. They operate from dawn until almost midnight. **Stations are marked by a large**

M sign and tickets can be bought at tobacco shops, newsstands and the station's ticket booth or vending machines. There are also daily tourist passes available. Unless you crave close body contact, I advise you to avoid the subways during the time of day when the locals are traveling to and from work because the subways tend to be even more crowded than the buses. You will need to move with speed if you're carrying luggage, and promptly get it out of the doorway.

~

I once watched a lady frantically try to extricate her little two-wheeled grocery carrier from the jaws of the subway doors. This brought back not-so-fond memories of the time I got my luggage cart stuck in the door tracks of the Paris subway, preventing them from closing and delaying departure of the car for what seemed like an eternity. It was during the morning rush, and I can't repeat some of the names the Parisians called me, the kindest of which was "idiote touriste Americaine."

~

Some towns in Italy have funiculars or inclines that take people to the surrounding hills or, such as in Capri, from the marina to the city center. If you don't mind heights, they are an efficient way to reach the top of the mountain and you can see some beautiful views in the process. Most have ticket booths or coin machines at each end.

BOATS

In certain places in Italy, the best, or sometimes the only way, to get there or get around is via water transportation.

Venice, of course, is the primary example of this. The streets comprise a series of canals surrounded by sidewalks and small alleys. There are only two ways to get around: by boat or on foot.

Venice's public transportation consists of motorboats (*vaporetti*) that act as water busses which travel

the Grand Canal from one end of Venice to the other. Tickets can be bought at the individual boat docks and vary in price, depending on the distance traveled. You can save money by buying a 24-hour or a 72-hour pass. Tickets are validated by scanning them against the machine located on the boarding platform.

The *diretto* only makes a few select stops; the *accellerato* makes all the stops. Neither is particularly fast, but the *vaporetti* are a cheap way to get around and an easy way to tour the Grand Canal. The boats are crowded from March through October, especially during summer week-ends, when along with the foreign tourists, the day trippers visit the city. **Vaporetto line No. 1 takes you from the train station (Santa Lucia) to St. Mark's Square (Piazza San Marco).** It's also a good way to admire the interesting architecture of the ancient buildings on the canal.

Since there are only three bridges crossing the Grand Canal, visitors must take a *traghetto* gondola to get across. They are located at various points along the canal at alleyways called Calle del Traghetto. Unlike regular gondola rides, the fare to get across is inexpensive (under $1.00).

Water taxis in Venice are extremely expensive (75 to 100 euros) and not always private, since the driver usually picks up more than one fare. But, if you're overloaded with suitcases, it may be the best way to go.

Gondola rides are highly romanticized and also expensive. The price is whatever you negotiate with the gondolier and increases in the evening. Whether you get your money's worth depends on the gondolier. It can be a memorable, romantic experience or a disaster.

~

My friends Winnie and Roger were strolling along one of the canals as the sun was setting. They watched another couple in a gondola, being serenaded by the gondolier, so they decided to book a ride. They paid the gondolier's asking price and then they relaxed in the gondola, anticipating a pleasant ride down the canal.

They were not as lucky as the couple they had observed. Their gondolier got into a tiff with a fellow gondolier and ended up arguing with him all the way down the canal. At one point, they were afraid that the altercation would turn physical and they would end up in the water along with their gondolier. This situation made the whole gondola experience very unpleasant for my friends, and left them with a less than favorable impression of Venice.

~

Italian lakes such as Lake Como, Garda and Maggiore, all have boat service that can be used as public transportation to get from city to city along the shore, or as a sightseeing tool to tour the lake. The cost is reasonable and an easy way to travel. Some cities also have speed boats *(motoscafi)* that take passengers quickly around the lake, which can be fun but will make it more difficult to admire the scenery than the slower boat.

~

While in Como, I took a slow boat ride to Bellagio, a small resort town on the lake. It was a pleasant, relaxed experience. I admired the villas and gardens along the lake as the vessel stopped at various quaint little towns. I chose to stop in Bellagio because it was advertised as being the most charming and it certainly was. I walked up the narrow paths, looked in the shops, and had a lovely lunch along the lake. It was a relaxing day.

The following afternoon, my brother arrived in Como and we took a speed boat tour of the lake. It was a fun, exciting ride, as the wind blew through our hair and the mist from the water sprayed our faces. We sped by the shores, and the driver pointed out the homes of the celebrities who lived in the area. As we approached George Clooney's residence, we spotted him standing on his boat dock. He waved and smiled good-naturedly as we yelled, "Hey George!"

~

To get to the islands, such as Capri and Sardinia, it's necessary to take a ferry (*traghetto*) or hydrofoil (*aliscafo*). There are also small towns on the Italian Riviera such as Portofino, and the cities that are part of the Cinque Terre area, that are best reached by boat. I find traveling on the water a pleasant and often more scenic diversion than other means of public transportation.

WALKING

In many Italian cities, you can cover the important sites on foot. Some even have pedestrian-only areas for eating or window shopping. To get around the major cities on foot, you need to be able-bodied, and move quickly and carefully while crossing the street. Vehicles don't always obey the speed limit and in some cities, drivers ignore traffic signals. They consider them only a suggestion.

Cross at the crosswalks when available and don't ever be tempted to jaywalk. My fellow Pittsburghers, who have a habit of crossing against the light and in the middle of the street, would not survive a day in Rome, much less in Naples.

The last time I was near the Rome train station, I couldn't get across the street even at the crosswalk until a man in his eighties stopped traffic with his cane and got us across while yelling obscenities at the inconsiderate drivers. It was an enlightening and humbling experience.

It is safest to stay on the sidewalk until you are ready to cross, and be particularly aware of motor scooters. They sway in and out of traffic with little regard for pedestrians, squeeze between cars, disregard crosswalks, and sometime even end up on the sidewalk.

The reason I emphasize walking safety is because one of my elderly relatives was killed by a speeding car when she stepped off the curb unexpectedly one evening.

DINING

Eating out in Italy is a heavenly experience. Every area has its local specialties made with fresh ingredients and prepared with pride. You will not find chain restaurants other than some of the American fast-food ones, which are mostly frequented by students, or Americans longing for a tall soda with ice or a cup of weak coffee. Dining out does not have to be a budget-busting event if you're careful.

Breakfast

Italians don't eat breakfast the way Americans do. Most chug a tiny shot of strong coffee prior to leaving for work, and if they eat anything at all, it's usually bread with butter or marmalade, a croissant or sweet roll.

In the last decade, I've noticed that most hotels have expanded their breakfast to satisfy the requirements of foreign tourists. In addition to the standard breads and pastries accompanied by coffee or tea, lately I've also found fruit, cheeses, lunch meats, boiled eggs and a few varieties of cereals along with juices. There are two items I have yet to see on any Italian hotel breakfast buffet table, though: scrambled eggs and my favorite cereal—Cheerios.

Breakfast is usually included in the room's price of most Italian hotels, although a few have started charging guests. If your hotel doesn't supply breakfast, you can always get coffee and a pastry at a local café. Italians consume their coffee standing at the counter; table service costs extra. Also, don't ask for "toast" unless you want a grilled ham and cheese sandwich.

My recent experience has been that the quantity and selection of breakfast items will vary from city to city and hotel to hotel without any correlation to the rating or room rate. The most abundant selection I have encountered was at a small hotel in Vicenza, where the room rate was only 57 euros per night (about $80 at the time).

Lunch and Dinner

As for your other meals, if you want to eat tasty, regional cuisine at reasonable prices, don't go where the tourists go--follow the locals. **You will usually find the best food in some unpretentious little *osteria* (small restaurant) on a** side street away from the tourist area. Go off the beaten path, find a place with a menu hand-written on a blackboard by the door, and that's where you will find the best meals without spending a fortune.

You could ask the personnel at your hotel desk to recommend a place to eat, but I don't always trust them. They may have a brother-in-law who owns a restaurant that they're trying to promote, or may send you to places they think a typical American would like, which may not be what you want. I usually follow someone who speaks the local dialect to see where they go. Of course, if you're in a city with many foreign tourists and can't distinguish Italian from Greek, then this may be more difficult.

I've also asked store clerks and people on the street to recommend a restaurant. Occasionally, I've consulted travel guides, but I mostly rely on the locals. Friends of mine who spent two weeks in Italy last year used the Rick Steves' travel book and were quite satisfied. I had dinner with them on a couple of evenings in Rome where we dined at places recommended by Mr. Steves. The restaurants were quite charming and served unique, tasty dishes.

MENUS

Many of these small places don't have menus in English, and some don't have menus at all. In that case, the waiter or proprietor, who may also be the chef, will recite the menu to you verbally. I have to admit that, even though I speak the language, sometimes it's difficult to comprehend and remember the selections. I often get the specialty of the house or ask the waiter what he or she recommends. I have never been disappointed.

You may find children's portions, but you're not likely to find children's menus. In Italy, children eat what their parents eat.

Many restaurants in cities frequented by tourists have menus in various languages.

Since the advent of the computer, I have come across some interesting translations. In one little Venetian restaurant, I found something on a menu listed as "rat fish."(It was supposed to be monk fish.) There were several other serious faux-pas on the menu that I couldn't resist bringing to the attention of the waiter. The manager asked me to make the corrections, thanked me profusely, and rewarded me with a free dessert.

Being bilingual has paid off on a couple of other occasions. In Siena, I watched the waiter struggle to explain the menu, via pantomime, to an Australian couple. After several minutes of amusement, I decided to offer my help.

I proceeded to play translator, then ended up having a pleasant conversation with the couple and getting a free carafe of wine.

Italian restaurants don't usually offer many selections, but their menu changes on a daily basis, and although they may feature the same local specialties, each restaurant has its own unique way of preparing the item.

Italians eat everything. You may find unusual game meats, rabbit, gnocchi with boar sauce, or items such as brains, tongue and intestines on the menu, some of which are considered delicacies. You may even occasionally find horse meat. **So, if you want to make sure you don't eat anything you will later regret, arm yourself with a translator.** One item I have seldom seen offered is chicken. I'm not sure exactly why, but it's not popular in Italian restaurants.

Unless you've opted for the *Menu Turistico* (Tourist Menu), items are usually served a la carte; however, on my most recent trip, I noticed many restaurants were adding a few grilled vegetables or potatoes on the plate, along with whatever fish or meat I ordered.

COURSES

The main meal is divided into four courses; most Italians order at least two.

Antipasto--the appetizer.

Primo—the first course, which consists of soup, pasta or risotto.

Secondo—the main dish of meat or fish. Side dishes that accompany the main dish are called *contorni*.

Dolce—the dessert, which besides a variety of pastries and ice cream, could also include a selection of cheeses.

Bread

Bread is served in a basket as soon as you sit down, along with your napkin and silverware, and is referred to *as Il Coperto* (the cover). The customer is billed extra for it whether he eats it or not. Although the cost only amounts to a few dollars, this practice seems to baffle and irritate many Americans. Over the years, my traveling companions have questioned me about the purpose for this extra charge, but I don't have a good explanation. That's just the way things are done in Italy.

The type of bread served varies from region to region, but butter is never included with it. Although Italians spread butter on the bread or rolls they eat at breakfast, they do not butter their dinner bread. They use the bread to clean up whatever residue of sauce is left on the plate.

Salads

A mixed salad, which is usually not included, is served either with or after the main entrée unless you request it to be served before—in which case the waiter will look at you as if you had two noses and shake his head before he brings it to you. Besides the standard leaf lettuce or radicchio, your salad can include some interesting items such as kidney beans, boiled potatoes, corn or hard-boiled eggs.

What you will get is always a surprise, so if you're not flexible, it's best to ask. Another popular item is a tomato or cucumber salad or a combination of the two. Although I have seen a small selection of salad dressings for sale in the supermarkets, all you will get in a genuine Italian restaurant is olive oil and vinegar (wine or balsamic). I hate to admit it, but I still seldom use the right proportions. My salad usually ends up too oily or too tart. If any of my relatives are with me, I ask them to season the salad for me.

Fish

Unless you specify otherwise, fish is usually served whole, head and all, which doesn't bother me, though it does disturb some people.

I ordered roasted orata (sea bass) in Venice when I was traveling with my friend Gerry, and the waiter presented it to me whole.

"Yuck! It still has the head on!" Gerry shrieked.

"That's OK. No big deal. That's the way they serve fish here."

She couldn't take her eyes off the fish. She stared at it as if it was going to jump up and bite her.

"I can't stand it. It's looking at me," she said.

"How can it be looking at you? It's dead."

"Please have the head removed," she begged. "It's bothering me."

I summoned the waiter, and pleaded with him to take the fish back to the kitchen and have its head removed because it was freaking out my friend.

Ice Cream and Pastries

You cannot leave Italy without tasting the delicious pastries (*paste*) for which each region is famous, and the ice cream (*gelato*). *Pasticerrie* (pastry shops) carry an array of delectable-looking goodies to satisfy your sweet tooth. The *gelato* is outstanding. I consume gallons of it every time I go.

There are *gelaterie* throughout the cities which display

their goodies in colorful, delicious-looking mounds that tempt you as you stroll through the streets. There's an array of flavors to rival Baskin and Robbins. My favorite is *nocciola* (hazelnut). I have yet to dislike any type of ice cream; however, if you want to ensure that you're getting genuine, homemade gelato, look for a sign that states "*gelato artigianale*."

OTHER PERTINENT DINING INFORMATION

Some familiar items are prepared differently in Italy. In many parts of the country, pasta is served with a very light amount of sauce, and lasagna, which in certain regions of Italy is called pasticcio, is made with a béchamel sauce instead of the thick tomato sauce popular here. In the south of Italy, you are more likely to find pasta dishes served the way we are used to eating them in the U.S.; however, even there, dishes will not be exactly the same.

Tomato sauce with ground meat is called *ragu* in Italy, and they don't usually serve spaghetti with meatballs. There are several other items that in the U.S. are prepared with tomato sauce, which may not be cooked that way in Italy. In Rome, I ate the most delicious eggplant parmesan I have ever tasted, but it didn't contain one drop of tomato sauce.

Pizza can be thick or thin, depending on the area, and is usually made with fresh mozzarella cheese. The selection of toppings is varied and interesting and, besides the traditional vegetables and meats, can include such items as ham and eggs. Be careful, though: **if you ask for pepperoni, you will probably end up with some type of peppers**.

Italian potato salad does not contain mayonnaise and is closer to the German version. If you ask for a ham-and-cheese *Panini*, you will get a long roll with cold ham and some type of white cheese. What we in Pittsburgh refer to as *panini* is called *tostato* or just *toast* in most parts of Italy. Sandwiches are called *tramezzini*.

When dining, you need to be adventurous and flexible. You may not always get what you think you've ordered, but the food will surely be tasty. Being a curious diner is considered a sign of sophistication. **Italian restaurants do not provide doggy bags.** Since the portions are smaller than in the U.S., leftovers are seldom an issue. Also, Italians consider taking home leftovers tacky. If they actually do have a pet with which they want to share their meal, they bring their own container, but this is seldom done.

Waiters will not ask you if you need anything else, or pester you to order more drinks. If you want something, you'll need to summon your server. You can sit at the table for as long as you wish and will not be presented with your check until you ask for it. This practice is followed regardless of whether you're having a full meal in a fancy restaurant or a cup of coffee in a café. The table is yours until you vacate it; this is one of the customs that appeals to me about dining in Europe.

The lack of attention from the server may be misinterpreted as aloofness or poor service by American tourists who are used to waiters hovering over them. After I get my meal, I prefer to be left alone, so the fact that my server ignores me until I call him is not a problem.

Don't be surprised if you hear a group at a table singing, or see someone playing cards after lunch or dinner. You will also spot senior citizens sitting in a café having their coffee and reading the paper well into mid-morning, while in mid-afternoon, ladies--sometimes with children in tow--will be having their afternoon coffee or aperitif. Then in the early evening, you will find the work crowd enjoying happy hour before going home for a late supper.

Europeans prefer to eat and drink outdoors whenever possible. Even in the dead of winter, you will come across people sitting at the outdoor tables of cafés sipping their coffee, hot chocolate, wine or brandy.

Don't be shocked if you're sitting at an outdoor restaurant and see a dog sitting peacefully at the foot of its owner, or a stray cat waiting patiently for handouts. Dogs are permitted in the outdoor areas of some establishments, and stray animals are often tolerated, especially in small towns.

Once upon a time, people used to get dressed-up to go to dinner, and patrons in jeans and tennis shoes were not admitted in certain restaurants. Recently, I've noticed that even the Italians are dressing-down, so most restaurants have a pretty relaxed dress code. The only exceptions are some restaurants located within the casinos; however, some restaurants may choose to keep out people who look particularly grubby--people wearing dirty, torn clothes. Shoes and shirt are a must everywhere.

Anyone handling food in Italy—from cook to store clerk—is required to be trained and certified.

FAST FOOD

The Golden Arches have managed to infiltrate Italy. Most major cities have at least one restaurant, usually at the train station, in a mall, or other shopping area. My friends have also told me that they spotted a couple of Burger Kings in Milan. I have seen Subway restaurants in other parts of Europe, but none in Italy yet. I suspect they will work their way south before my next visit.

If you need a fix of burgers and fries or soda with ice, you'll be happy to know that the McDonald's in Italy serve basically the same food as the ones at home. The only difference is that they carry more interesting desserts, and some serve wine and beer along with their soft drinks. My coffee-drinking friends tell me that the locations where coffee is served have excellent cappuccino and espresso, but you can't get any drinks "to go."

If you're looking for a cheap meal like you find in the States, though, you won't find it at the McDonald's in Europe. Their prices are considerably higher than here.

McDonald's is mostly frequented by students and

tourists. Italian adults looking for fast food usually prefer the *tavola calda* (hot table), where pre-cooked, take-out meals consisting of the local cuisine can be purchased, or they pick up their dinners at the prepared-food section of the supermarkets.

DINING UTENSILS

Tablespoons in Italy are much larger than ours, while teaspoons are very tiny. Since restaurants don't serve butter with their bread, they don't always provide butter knives. You will find cute little ice cream spoons that look like mini shovels, which I have purchased for myself and other family members. Besides ice cream, they are also useful for eating cantaloupe or watermelon. Cereal bowls and plates are smaller than ours, and so are cups. My cousin only had tiny coffee cups in her apartment, and since I'm a tea drinker, I bought a couple of mugs that she keeps for me.

DINING HOURS, CREDIT CARDS, AND TIPPING

Most restaurants are open for two to three hours (11 or 11:30 a.m. to 2 or 2:30 p.m.) for lunch and for three or four hours (7 or 7:30 p.m. to 11 or 11:30 p.m.) for dinner. The idea of set dining hours is another custom that is difficult for Americans to accept.

~

"What do you mean we can't eat at 5 o'clock?" my friend Janice asked me on her first visit to Europe.

"I'm hungry now," she said as we passed a restaurant that looked appealing.

"This restaurant doesn't open until 7:30; Europeans eat late. We can have a drink and some snacks in a bar or café in the meantime, but nothing will be open for dinner anywhere before 7 o'clock."

"That's stupid. You mean no one here eats dinner before 7 o'clock?"

"They eat a bigger lunch than we do...and the women often

stop at the grocery store after work to buy the fresh food they're going to cook for dinner. That's the way they do things in Europe."
By the end of the trip, she had adjusted to the late dining hours.

~

That was a couple of decades ago when absolutely nothing was open between 2:30 p.m. and 7 p.m. Now, in the popular cities, some restaurants that cater to tourists are open continuously. In those places, you will usually get food of the type you find in an Italian restaurant in the States, or the type of meal many Americans are used to eating at home. The food may be tasty, but most likely won't be the authentic local cuisine found in the quaint little establishments that are only open during regular dining hours. **Some restaurants are closed on Sundays, Mondays or both.**

Restaurants and bars located near major attractions are more expensive than those in other parts of town, some exorbitantly so. I paid the equivalent of $10 for a beer near Il Duomo in Florence, and $12 for two scoops of ice cream at a café in St. Mark's square in Venice.

Many restaurants don't accept the American Express Credit card, or traveler's checks. Some of the smaller restaurants don't accept credit cards at all, so be sure to bring euros. (Some used to accept dollars, but since the devaluation of our currency, most no longer do.)

Restaurants do not usually issue separate checks for a group.

Tipping guidelines are different than in the States. Tipping is not customary in bars or cafes, but if a patron is consuming food along with his drink, he sometimes leaves the change. I've found that if you do leave even a small tip when you order a drink, you will get prompter service and extra munchies the next time you show up.

In restaurants, Italians tip from 5% to 12%, depending on the type of meal, the amount of time spent in the restaurant, and the service provided. If you're in a group, some restaurants automatically add a gratuity. If you see "*servizio*" on your bill, it means the tip was add-

ed. You can leave extra cash if the service was good.

~

I had taken my cousin Clelia and her husband to dinner in a nice restaurant in Trieste, and after consuming a three-course meal, a bottle of wine and some after dinner drinks, I received a bill totaling 79 euros. The food was delicious and our service was good, so I handed the waitress 100 euros and told her to keep the change. She returned a couple of minutes later. She had a baffled look on her face.

"Signora, I think you made a mistake. You gave me too much money," she said, in Italian.

"No. It's OK. It's your tip," I said.

"Oh no, Signora. It's too much."

"What did you do?" my cousin Clelia asked me. "Are you being an American again? How much of a tip did you give her?"

"About 20%, like I do at home."

"Are you insane?! We don't do that here," my cousin informed me, shaking her head.

"What do you normally get?" I asked the waitress. She kept 5 euros and returned the rest. We were there several hours, and I felt she deserved more, but she wouldn't accept it.

The next time I ate there, though, she sat me at the best table despite the fact that I was alone. I left her a 20% tip and ran out the door before she could protest.

Servers in Italy welcome tipping, but they don't expect it or depend it on it, as they do in the U.S. That's one of the reasons they don't rush customers, or push drinks.

WATER & OTHER BEVERAGES

I've never had a problem with the water in Italy and although the taste is not unpleasant, most Italians drink bottled water—either plain (*naturale*), or carbonated (*frizzante*). **If you want tap water with ice, ask for *aqua del rubinetto con ghiaccio*, otherwise you will be served bottled water. Italians drink almost everything at room temperature without ice.** Many also drink wine with every meal except breakfast. Although the drinking age in Italy is eighteen, restaurants will serve wine to children if the parents permit it (not to toddlers, of course).

When I was a child in Italy, my parents used to serve me *due-ditti*--two fingers' worth of wine in a glass mixed with water or fruit juice at dinner. It was considered healthy. I still drink a glass every day with my main meal. It enhances my enjoyment of the food and helps my digestion.

Wine is relatively inexpensive in Italy. I found that the house wine in restaurants is quite satisfactory because it's usually a regional wine bought in bulk directly from the vineyard of the producer. It's served by the liter, which is approximately a quart. You can get a half-liter or quarter-liter carafe. Some places will serve wine by the individual glass, but it's usually more advantageous to buy a small carafe. If you want something fancier, you can also buy a bottle of wine produced in Italy for a reasonable price.

Although most Italians consume wine with their meals, they do like beer with their pizza or snacks, especially on a hot summer day. They also enjoy an *aperitivo* (aperitif) and *digestivo* (digestive) before and after dinner. The types vary from region to region and could be alcoholic or not *(analcaolico)*.

The popular aperitif throughout Italy during my last visit was something called Aperol Spritz, which was a concoction of dry, sparkling, white wine *(prosecco)*, seltzer and a bitter orange liqueur called Aperol. The after dinner drink could be something strong like grappa, brandy or cognac; or lighter like Sambuca or Limoncello (a liqueur made from lemons), or an *amaro* (bitter). My favorite is egg cognac, a very-sweet liqueur I was allowed to sample as a child.

Although Italians like their alcohol, most consume it in moderation with meals and to socialize--not for the sole purpose of getting drunk. The only staggering-drunk people I have encountered in the thirty years I've traveled through Italy, besides a couple of old derelicts, were tourists.

~

I was walking around town after a rock concert one summer

evening and expected to encounter drunken young people behaving badly, but I didn't see the type of conduct I have witnessed outside some popular bars in Pittsburgh on an average Saturday night. *No one was staggering or throwing up on the street, and outside of a rather intense public display of affection by a young couple and some animated conversations, everyone was rather subdued--at least by Pittsburgh's standards. Maybe the fact that Italian children are exposed to wine at an early age might make them less likely to overindulge when they become young adults.*

~

You won't find an extensive selection of sodas in all restaurants or bars. There is orange soda, Coca-Cola, *gingerino* and a few other choices, including diet soda. Italians favor bottled juices such as grapefruit (*pompelmo*) and lemonade (*limonata*). In places that cater to tourists, there will be a larger selection of American beverages, but they are more expensive than the local sodas. You can buy Coke, but I have not seen Pepsi. The Coke will cost substantially more than in the U.S., especially in a restaurant. If you must have soda, the local products are tasty and much less expensive than American brands.

When my friend Janice and I were in Rome, along with my teen-aged niece and Janice's pre-teen nephew, we ordered a bottle of wine and a couple of Cokes to go with our pizza. The most expensive item was the children's Cokes; they cost more than the bottle of wine.

The same applies to hard liquor. Brands popular in America can be found in Italy, but the price for a drink will usually be higher than in most States.

The real Italian addiction is coffee. They chug it early in the morning for breakfast, usually have another cup mid-morning and mid-afternoon. They often also consume it after lunch and dinner. Italian coffee is very strong, looks like molasses, and is served in tiny cups. I'm not usually a coffee drinker, since American coffee destroys my stomach and gives me the jitters, but in Italy I occasionally sip a small cup of *macchiato* (coffee with a dollop of cream) without repercussions.

The terminology for the various types of coffees in Italy is different from ours. If you ask for *latte*, you will get plain milk. If you want what Starbucks sells as *latte*, you will have to ask for *caffe-latte*. The regular type of coffee you drink at home in the morning is called *caffè Americano or caffè lungo*, although people have told me it's not quite the same as ours. You can also get decaf *(decaffinato)*, if you ask for it.

Not many people drink tea on a regular basis. It's considered medicinal and mostly consumed to soothe the stomach—with lemon, never with cream. I prefer decaffeinated tea and usually bring my own because it's hard to find in the stores. Herbal tea, which is called *tizana*, has recently gained some popularity.

You will find iced coffee being served in cafes and restaurants during the summer, but you will not find iced tea. I never noticed it until my friend Linda, who is an avid iced-tea drinker, pointed it out to me. If you really want iced tea, they will brew it for you and then serve it with ice, but it won't be the pre-prepared version that you find in restaurants in the States.

Italian hot chocolate is outstanding. Some places make it so thick you can actually stand a spoon in it. It is even served with additional hot milk, in case you want to water it down.

COOKING & GROCERY SHOPPING

If you're preparing your own meals, you will find grocery shopping easy and fun even if you don't speak the language. There are now supermarkets available in most Italian cities; however, people still prefer to grocery shop in the small specialty stores. Every day, the shoppers grab their canvas or plastic grocery bags and head to market. They stop at the butcher shop or fishery, the fruit and vegetable market, the delicatessen, and the bakery.

Some cities have an outdoor or indoor market that operates year-round, where most of the cook's requirements can be found. A couple of times a week, shoppers visit the supermarket or other stores to get their packaged items, paper products, cleaning supplies, and other household needs. This sounds very complicated and time-consuming, but it really isn't. When I stay at my cousin's apartment, I hop on the 9:00 a.m. bus for the eight-minute ride to town, buy meat or fish, fruit, vegetables and bread, and am back home by 10:30. That's usually less time than it takes me to go to my supermarket in Pittsburgh.

Grocery shopping is an enlightening experience. Things have changed since I lived in Italy as a child, but not by much. When I used to shop for my mother back in those days, I would tell the grocer how much of an item I wanted, and he used to weigh it, roll up some brown paper into a cone, and place my purchase inside. Now, many have automated scales.

~

On my first visit to a market, about a decade ago, I watched one of the local ladies to figure out the process. She put on a pair of disposable plastic gloves taken from a dispenser, pulled a plastic bag from another dispenser, and headed for the tomatoes. She picked a few, placed them in the bag, walked over to the scale, pushed a button, and a sticker with the price popped out. It seemed simple enough, but how did the scale know the price of the item she was buying? I had to watch several people before I figured it out.

~

There is a number in front of the bin where each type of produce is stored which corresponds to numbers on the scale. When the number is punched, the correct price pops out. What a simple process. I'm sure some devious person could find a way to cheat the system, but I watched most cashiers surreptitiously check the content of the bag against the label to insure that they matched. I've heard some supermarkets in the U.S. now use that system also, but it hasn't reached Pittsburgh yet.

When I'm in Italy, I usually frequent the same markets, and after being there a few weeks, they got to know me.

I told them I was visiting from America, and they guided me in the way of Italian shopping.

~

I was buying plums one day, and the grocer asked me: "Are you planning to eat those or make marmalade?"

"I'm going to eat them."

"Then you don't want those; they're not ripe enough to eat. Come back tomorrow; we'll have good edible ones then."

What did I know? They looked good enough to me—certainly better than any of the ones I find in Pittsburgh.

Every few days, I bought a bunch of bananas.

"You really like your bananas," the grocer commented after a couple of weeks.

"They're my medicine. I have to eat one a day for potassium."

One day, I got to the store late, and all the bananas were gone. The vendor saw me looking around.

"Don't worry," the grocer said, "I figured you were due to buy bananas, so I saved some for you."

On the last day I was in town, he also saved me a couple of figs because the day before I had told him I would be in for my last taste of figs.

He wasn't the only vendor who looked out for me.

Early one morning, I went to the fish market to buy some sardoni, a local fish similar to sardines.

"I want to warn you that these aren't fresh. They're from yesterday, but if you really want them, I'll give them to you at half price," the merchant said.

"That's fine. Where I come from, yesterday's fish is considered a good thing. We're lucky if it's less than a week old," I said.

"Che peccato (What a pity)," he mumbled as he wrapped my fish.

You don't get that type of personal touch at Giant Eagle or Walmart.

~

When grocery shopping in Italy, it's important to remember that items are sold and priced by the kilogram, which equates to roughly two pounds.

If you want a picnic lunch, and don't feel like making too many stops, it's easy to go to the supermarket, purchase a few ounces of lunch meat or cheese, a roll, some fruit, and even a bottle of wine. To make it simple instead of trying to figure out the quantity required, you can ask for *un pocco per due panini* (a little for two sandwiches) when ordering deli meat, or get some pre-packaged items from the cold food section.

You will find many American products in Italy, but they may not be exactly the same because there are certain additives, preservatives and food colorings that are banned there, and although their parent company may be in the U.S., they often are manufactured in Europe with ingredients that may vary slightly from ours.

There are very few salad dressings available in the supermarkets, and although there is a large selection of cheeses, cheddar is not among them.

~

During one of my trips, I was trying to make a Mexican dish to serve to my Italian relatives and couldn't find any cheddar cheese.

"You guys don't have any of our American yellow cheese," I commented to my cousin.

"Probably because people had enough of it after the war," she said, jokingly.

When the Americans occupied Italy towards the end of WWII and food was scarce, they distributed cheddar cheese, among other things, to the locals.

~

I don't know the real reason for the unavailability of cheddar cheese, but I've never seen it in either supermarkets or dairy stores.

Supermarkets and other grocery stores sell liquor, although their selection may not be as extensive as in the liquor stores. Bakeries often sell milk. **Eggs are not refrigerated** because they are very fresh; they were probably still in the chicken the day before.

Expiration dates are firm (the dates are written as

day, month, year). If your milk carton states that it's due to expire on 3/6/12, don't attempt to drink it on June 3, or you will be spending the rest of the day in the bathroom. I know this from personal experience. Their fresh milk only lasts a few days, but there's also milk available that has been processed to last longer. The carton will state: *a lunga conservazione*. I don't like the taste of it so I only use it in my cereal.

Because fresh products spoil quickly and storage in people's homes is at a premium, Italians purchase small quantities and shop often. Things are packaged for cramped storage—no mega rolls or extra-large sizes.

Although I hate grocery shopping in the States, I actually enjoy shopping in Italy.

ENTERTAINMENT

Visitors can learn what's happening in any city from the tourist office, the local paper, or from the city's website.

During the warm-weather months, many towns feature free entertainment in the squares on weekends and even during the week. You will also find a variety of music which appeals to all tastes in bars throughout the cities. Discos and other establishments that cater to the younger crowd are open until 4 or 5 in the morning. Anywhere there is music, you will find people of all ages congregating. Concerts, musicals, and plays are staged in regular theaters, castles, stadiums, or the remains of Roman amphitheaters.

Theaters feature both international and local artists. You can see some of the same musicals that tour in the States performed in the original English language. Prices to attend cultural events are much cheaper than in the U.S.

Opera is big in Italy. Performances in the major opera houses such as *La Scala* in Milan and *La Fenice* in Venice have to be booked well in advance. If you plan to attend a performance, you will need formal clothes: at least a dark suit and tie for men and a fancy dress for women.

Very few of the movies shown in Italy are produced there. Movie theaters feature mostly American films, some dubbed and some in English with Italian subtitles. There are also German and French pictures.

There are special festivals that take place throughout Italy during the year. You can find a list of these on the internet (Italy festivals) or the city's website. The information is in English. Most cities celebrate Mardigras with costumes and floats, and summer festivals featuring art, music, dancing and other cultural events performed outdoors.

Besides a Mardigras extravaganza that rivals New Orleans and Rio, **Venice** holds a film festival that attracts numerous stars in early September, gondola races, regattas and other festivities throughout the summer. There is also the Biennale International Art Festival every other year.

Florence has an Easter Festival, music and art festivals during the spring and summer, and wine festivals and antique fairs in the fall.

Rome holds open air performances throughout the summer, and a grape festival with folk entertainment in the fall.

Cities celebrate the feast of their patron saint. There is a mass and procession to honor the saint, in addition to more secular activities such as eating, drinking and dancing. There are also religious celebrations from Palm Sunday to Easter Sunday. During the month of December, many cities hold a Christmas market that includes entertainment. On December 31, New Year's Eve is celebrated with music and fireworks.

In the summer, the Catholic churches hold festivals (*sagras*) that feature food, drinks, and music that ranges from folk to popular. They are similar to the church festivals held in the U.S., but more geared towards adults.

~

On two occasions, I attended the festival at the Church of San Lorenzo in Trieste, where I worshipped as a child. Every night, there was live entertainment featuring different genres of music. The church ladies served local food specialties that consisted of grilled meats and fish, along with potatoes, vegetables, dessert, wine, beer, and water. For 10 euros (about $13), I ate a full meal, drank two glasses of wine, danced and sang.

One night, a group was playing a combination of Italian pop music, rock-and-roll, and American country-western tunes. The female singer noticed I was tapping my feet and lip-syncing to the songs.

"Do you know any country-western dances?" she asked me.

I confessed I knew a few, so she asked me to come up and help her teach the audience some basic steps. She gathered a few brave souls, and she and I demonstrated a country version of the Electric Slide, and a couple of other simple country classics.

By the end of the evening, most of the audience, including senior citizens, were dancing on the concrete floor. I had a great time.

~

Besides stopping for an aperitif or coffee, another favorite Italian pastime is *"la passegiata"* (the promenade). After dinner, the locals put on their best clothes, parade around the main squares, waterfront or lakefront, and then stop for cocktails or ice cream.

On Sunday, the promenade starts after lunch and lasts until late into the evening. It's an opportunity to see and be seen, meet friends and neighbors, hook-up with members of the opposite sex and even get some exercise. This can be fun, especially on the weekend, when there is usually music emanating from the various establishments around the city.

CASINOS

Gamblers will find casinos in a few Italian cities. The main ones are in Lido, an island near Venice, and San Remo, on the Italian Riviera. There is also one located in the small town of Campione d'Italia, an Italian enclave located on Lake Lugano in Switzerland and another outside of Torino. Italian casinos are more glamorous than the ones I've seen in the States. You won't see senior citizens in polyester pants and tennis shoes gambling away their social security.

When I went to the casino in San Remo, a number of years ago, they still had a strict dress code: men were required to wear jackets and ties; women had to wear dress clothes. I wore a short, silk dress—the type I would wear to a wedding—and felt underdressed. Many of the patrons were in black-tie attire. Some fellow travelers who visited the casino in Venice within the last couple of years, informed me women are now permitted to wear slacks there, though jeans are still taboo.

Things change from year to year, and Italians are drifting towards American casualness in attire, but if you are planning to visit a casino, bring dress clothes just in case. Most casinos charge an entrance fee, and the gambling age in Italy is eighteen.

I have also heard that in certain cities there are clubs or bars that feature slot machines, card games or bingo games. I can't guarantee the legality of those establishments, so before you enter verify with your hotel staff what is legitimate. Just like in the States, laws and rules change, so check before you get into trouble. You don't want to have to pay a hefty fine or end up in an Italian jail.

SPORTS
Spectator Sports

The number one spectator sport in Italy is soccer (*calcio*), which they also call *futbol*. Most major cities have a team representing them, and Italians are as fanatical about soccer as Americans are about their football. **Other popular sports are cycling and car racing.** The most important bicycle race, Il *Giro d'Italia*, takes place in the late spring, and in September, you can view the Italian Grand Prix at Monza on Lake Como.

Hiking and Biking

If you're interested in activities such as hiking or biking, you can find clubs that will organize an excursion for you. Up-to-date information is available on the internet or sports publications.

Tennis and Golf

Although there are facilities for those sports, playing tennis or golf is difficult in Italy because membership to a club is usually required in order to participate. So, unless you know someone who belongs and is willing to invite you as a guest, you're out of luck.

Winter Sports

For skiers and other winter sports enthusiasts, there are many large and small ski resorts in the Alps and Dolomites. The most famous of these is Cortina d'Ampezzo, where the winter Olympics were held in the 1950s. You will also find a few resorts in the Apennines and the hills of Sicily.

Since I'm athletically challenged and don't like the cold, I have never skied in Italy, but people who do have found it to be a great experience and cheaper than skiing in the States. Even people like me can find something to do at a ski resort, though. Many are equipped with hot tubs or indoor pools and have après-ski activities to please non-skiers. You can always sit by the fire, sip hot toddies or mulled wine, and watch the beautiful scenery. Ski resorts are also good hiking destinations during the summer.

Swimming and Water Sports

Since Italy is surrounded by the sea, there are plenty of beaches where people can swim and, during the summer, many seaside or lakeside locations rent boats and water equipment for travelers interested in water sports.

The beaches of Italy are some of the most diverse in the world. You will encounter beautiful white sand like you would find in the Caribbean, as well as the rare black sand of the Sicilian beaches. There are also beaches covered with stones that can vary in size from tiny pebbles to large boulders. Each offers different panoramas, atmosphere, and amenities.

No matter which beach you pick, it will be crowded in July and August when the Italians, and half the population of Northern Europe, invade them. Weather permitting, the best time to hit the beach is late May, June or early September. Most beaches open after Easter and close in the middle of September; a few stay open into October. Some of the beaches open to the public are free, while others charge a fee. There are usually chair rentals and cabanas available for lease.

One important tip: if you are headed for any of the stony beaches, get yourself a pair of rubber beach shoes. I keep a pair at my cousin's apartment because my dainty feet can't handle the stony beaches of Trieste.

~

"Do you want to borrow my beach shoes?" my mother asked me before my first summer trip to Italy, back when I was young and vain. "You're going to need them at the beach."

"No thanks. I'll be fine." I wasn't going to wear those ugly rubber things. They wouldn't have looked cool with my new bikini.

My relatives took me to the beach, and I watched my cousin Michela, who was sixteen at the time, gracefully walk on the pebbles like a circus performer on a tight rope. I can do that, I thought as I attempted to follow her into the water. After executing several gyrations in an attempt to maintain my balance, I promptly fell on my butt.

"I think you better wear these," one of my older relatives suggested, pulling a pair of beach shoes out of her bag. I had to humbly accept.

"How do you guys do that? Those stones hurt and are slippery."

"We're used to it," they replied.

They must have developed a stratum of leather-like protection on the soles of their feet. I tried walking on the stones on several other occasions, all with the same result. Now, the shoes have become part of my beach wardrobe.

You can find various types of shoes anywhere beach supplies are sold in Italy, or you can buy them in the States. Just make sure that they have a sturdy bottom and stay on your feet. Flip-flops and crocs do not work. (Beach attire will be discussed further in the Etiquette and Italian Way of Life section, p. 130.)

Many of the lakes have beaches where people can swim as well as participate in water sports. Some hotels are equipped with swimming pools, most of which are located in resort areas or beach towns, but public pools are difficult to find in Italy. There are a few gyms with indoor pools, but most require membership.

TELEVISION

If you are staying in Italy long enough to care what's on television and you speak the language, you will find many American programs from previous seasons or past decades dubbed in Italian. It felt rather strange watching Castle and the Cosby kids speaking Italian in a voice that wasn't theirs. You may also catch decent movies from various countries besides Italy, and some good documentaries. The local news is on at 8 p.m., which is Italian dinner time, so what would be considered our primetime programs don't begin until 9 p.m. or later.

There is something of which tourists should be aware, though: Italians are more casual about nudity than we are in the United States, so, if you don't want your children or anyone else seeing scantily clad folks or bare-breasted women on the tube, stick to CNN and don't let the kids play with the remote.

During one visit to Italy, I was watching the evening news, and the newscaster was covering a serious car accident where the vehicle ended up on the beach. One of the witnesses was a topless bather, who was nonchalantly being interviewed on prime-time television. Also, some of television's late evening game shows may include scantily clad showgirls they call "*veline*," and on the weekend, you could run across some soft-porn programs on the local channels.

One great thing is that commercials are usually only shown at the beginning and end of a program without interrupting the show, and since they are usually much more creative and entertaining than ours, people actually stick around to watch them instead of running to the bathroom or the refrigerator.

ESPN addicts will go into withdrawal in Italy since American sports are not usually available on most hotels' television channels. If you're in an area that caters to tourists, though, you may find a bar that carries football or baseball games.

In Rome, one of my friends actually found a Steeler bar and I passed an Irish Pub that advertised American football live on their widescreen television. I don't remember who was scheduled to play on that Monday night but, because of the time difference, the game was going to air at 2 a.m. If I hadn't had to catch a flight that morning, I may have been tempted to go see who showed up to watch it.

SIGHT SEEING

Where you want to go and what you want to see will depend on your interests. The only tips I will offer are the following:

In the popular cities the best time of the day to go sight-seeing, especially if you're planning to take pictures, is either early in the morning or at dusk. If you want a photo of St. Mark's Square without having a woman with a flag and a bunch of strangers in your background, go while the tourists are having breakfast. If you long to sip a glass of *prosecco* at Café Florian and listen to symphony music without being distracted by children chasing pigeons, go during the dinner hour (between 7 and 9 p.m.).

If you can, try to avoid being in Venice or any small town when there are several cruise ships in port. (I actually check the major cruise lines' websites to see what days they are in Venice, so I can try to avoid them). There is nothing worse than being in Venice when there are several ships dumping thousands of tourists on its narrow streets. This is also the case for other popular stops like Portofino, Capri, Sorrento and Taormina

In Rome, I wandered around Piazza Navona early one morning, and strolled by the Coliseum at 7 p.m. It was lovely not to have to fight my way through a crowd. Other tourists were there, but in a tolerable number.

Arm yourself with a map and go off the beaten path. Travel to the back streets of Rome and Florence, and the tiny alleys along the canals of Venice. Instead of being elbow to elbow with a bunch of other tourists, you may discover some interesting architecture, little bridges and squares, and probably come across some quaint little *osteria* where you can eat lunch. I discovered a small square in Venice bearing the same name as my maternal great-grandfather. The square turned out to actually have been named after one of my ancestors, who had been a war hero.

Another important thing about sight-seeing: you can buy tickets in advance and make an appointment to visit some of the attractions in Italy, so you don't have to wait in long lines. This can be done on their website prior to departure, or through your hotel or local tourist office. If you plan to visit the Sistine Chapel, though, be prepared to wait in line even if you have a reservation.

If you want to see the Pope when he's in Rome, he gives a public audience every Wednesday beginning at 10:30 a.m. in the Paul VI Hall of Audiences, St. Peter's Basilica, or St. Peter's Square. You will need a ticket to attend. The free ticket can be obtained from the Prefecture of the Papal Household on Monday or Tuesday, or you can write ahead to: Prefecture of the Papal Household, Citta del Vaticano 00120 Italia. You must list the date you want to attend, the number of tickets required, and the language you speak. If you include the name of the hotel where you will be staying, the tickets will be sent there the afternoon before the audience.

The pope blesses visitors gathered in St. Peter's Square from his window on Sundays at noon, except during some of the summer months, when he's in his summer residence at Castel Gandolfo,

If you're visiting important cities with many attractions, I recommend you take a half-day city tour and then return to the places where you want to spend more time. Your hotel or the tourist office can help you with the tour arrangements.

When spending a few days in any of the large cities, it's easy and cheap to take a day-trip to a nearby location; just pick-up a schedule for the local trains or busses at the station, and decide where you want to go. From Milan, a twenty-minute train ride will take you to Lake Como, and in less than an hour, you can be visiting one of the other lakes. In two hours or less, you can get from Venice to Vicenza, Verona, Padua, Trieste or some of the little mountain towns in the Veneto region. It is easy to get from Florence to Siena, Pisa or Assisi or to visit one of the small Tuscan villages. The ruins of Ostia Antica are less than a forty–minute train ride from Rome.

From Rome you can also take a side-trip to Pompeii, Sorrento, Capri, Naples and the Amalfi coast, if you have a few extra days at your disposal. For this particular excursion, I would recommend an escorted tour since there are several means of transportation required to get to those places. Also, you have to pass through Naples which is a somewhat chaotic and intimidating city.

SHOPPING

Italy has very few malls, which are mostly located in the suburbs. The average Italians do their shopping downtown at specialty shops, and each city has one or more shopping areas. **There are several major department stores in**

Italy: *La Rinascente, Coin, Upim, OVS and Zara*.
La Rinascente is the most upscale of the group. It is on the caliber of Nordstrom or Sacks. Coin, Upim and OVS are all owned by the same company. Coin is the most upscale of the three and carries the type of merchandise found in our department stores. Upim, the oldest department store in Italy, has a variety of items for the entire family at reasonable prices. OVS (formerly known as Oviesse) sells low-priced quality items. Their products equate to the type of merchandise found at J.C. Penney's and Sears.

The newest department store to arrive in Italy is the Spanish chain store Zara.

Standa carries the type of merchandise sold at Target, except they do not sell food, cleaning supplies or paper products. The numerous shops and boutiques in the cities carry clothes, shoes and accessories of the type sold at Sacks, Talbot, Ann Taylor, and other more upscale stores found in American malls. **Designers such as Gucci, Armani, Versace and others distribute their fashions mostly through their own stores which are located in the major cities.**

Italian department stores don't feature the ample selection that stores in the United States do, and you will not find the same outfit in all sizes. Their plus sizes, which they tactfully refer to as *taglie commode* (comfortable sizes), are not as ample as ours and there are few extra-large selections available. Since there aren't many seriously obese people in Italy, finding clothes to fit an extra-large person is difficult. There may be a few items available in the touristy areas, but chances are they are not made in Italy.

Don't be misled by the labels. Clothes manufactured in Italy tend to be form-fitting, and sizes run smaller than ours. (I normally wear a medium top, but have to buy a large in Italy.) This applies to men's clothes as well as to women's. I also noticed that children's clothes seem to be a bit longer than ours.

When I was young and wore a size 6, I had no problem buying clothes in Italy, but now that I'm a 10 petite, it's more challenging since Italian stores don't seem to carry petite sizes. In Italian sizes, I wear anything from a 42 to a 46. I have better luck with Italian shoes, despite the fact that stores don't carry half sizes.

A size chart can be found in the Appendix (p.140), but use it only as a guide. Clothes and shoes produced in Italy are made of high quality materials and fashioned with superior craftsmanship. Be careful, though, some products made in China and Taiwan have found their way into the less prestigious department stores. I have also seen an increase in establishments run by questionable people selling cheap-looking goods.

Italian cities are a shopper's paradise. Their dazzling window displays entice you to buy. Clothes are overall expensive, but you can find some real bargains during the end-of-the-season sales (*saldi; svendita*) that are usually held in January and July. Young children's clothes are ridiculously pricey and, in my opinion, not as cute as ours. (I always bring clothes for my relatives' children because we have a larger selection, and our clothes are more practical.)

You can get elegant, beautifully-crafted leather goods for what we would pay for simpler items here. The biggest bargain in Italy, though, is jewelry—especially gold. Most of the gold sold there is 18 carats and, even with the unfavorable exchange rate, at least 30% cheaper than in the States. Their pieces are exquisitely designed and unique.

A few years ago, I bought a lovely pair of 18-carat, gold earrings for 85 euros (about $110 at the time). The same type of design and quality would have cost twice as much in the U.S.

Another item that is worth purchasing is fabric, especially drapery and other decorative material. The shops feature attractive designs and textures at prices comparable or cheaper than ours. My mother used to return from her visits to our relatives with a suitcase full of drapery material. Every curtain in her house is made of Italian fabric--curtains that have lasted for decades.

Hand-made lace is also an Italian specialty. You can find lovely tablecloths, doilies and other linens. Making lace is a skill that has been passed on from generation to generation and is still practiced in Italy.

~

My great-aunt Rosina was a skilled lace-maker. I still have the intricate pieces she gave me to use as trim for my sheets and pillow cases, back when I was in my twenties. She told me to: "put them away in your hope chest for when you get married." The lace has been sitting in my sewing drawer, lovingly preserved for several decades. I haven't had the heart to part with it, and I feel almost sacrilegious using it for a purpose other than the one for which she had intended it. Maybe I'll buy some white cotton sheets, attach the lace, and give them to my teen-aged grand-niece to start her hope chest.

~

In many cities, you can also purchase unique housewares, carved wood, ceramics and pottery, though some of it can be quite expensive.

Fine chocolate candy is a bargain in Italy. Once you've tasted their chocolate, you'll never crave a Hershey kiss again. Be careful what type of candy you feed your children, though. Some of it is filled with brandy, cognac or whiskey. The box will state (*ripieni di liquore*) or something to that effect, or list the specific type of liqueur. If the candy is wrapped individually, the name of the liqueur will appear on the wrapper.

Of course, if you want to ensure your children sleep on the flight home, stuffing their faces with booze-filled candy would be a good way to do that, since the liquor is potent.

~

I used to bring some of the candy to the office. The minute I put it out, my coworkers pounced on it like rabbits in a field of carrots. By noon, half of the staff was tipsy. The first time I deposited the candies in a basket outside my office, I neglected to warn a non-drinker, who loved chocolate, that it had liquor in it. She ate several pieces, and couldn't figure out what was happening to her when she started to fall asleep at

her desk.
   One of my bosses requested that I not put the candy out until after lunch. (He didn't consider banning the goodies because he consumed his fair share).

~

Bargaining at the markets is acceptable and expected (except at food markets). No haggling is usually done at department stores or specialty shops, of course. Store clerks, especially in jewelry stores, may offer you a discount if you are buying several items, though.

If you're interested in designer items, the best city to visit is Milan, since it's the home of high fashion, but you can find designer stores in all of the other major cities.

~

I've never bought designer items; I'm too practical and thrifty, and feel pretentious wearing them. In fact, I recently gave away a very expensive Gucci scarf that I had received as a gift, and which had been sitting in a box in my dresser drawer for over a decade.

The few times I've worn designer items that had been given to me, I felt I should be wearing a sign on my back that said: "Hey, I didn't buy it." So I'm not an authority on designers, however below is information on where you can purchase such items.

~

The following is a brief summary of shopping in the major cities. For further, up-to-date details, check the internet or the local tourist information desk:

Milan

There's a square area around the streets of Montenapoleone, Via della Spiga, Via Manzoni, and Via Sant'Andrea where the designers are located. There are also shops that sell designer items at a discount (Salvagente, Biffi, and Entrata Libera).

The Galleria Vittorio Emanuele, on the street by the same name, is one of the oldest indoor shopping areas. The gallery is covered with an impressive vaulted roof made of metal and glass, culminating in a splendid central dome. The floor is decorated with mosaic tiles.

Other than stores, it houses cafés, restaurants and bars. Burger King has also recently found a home there. The Galleria is close to Milan's famous *duomo*, and a great place to relax while shopping. It's one of my favorite stops when I'm in Milan.

For bargains, head for the area around the Brera Museum. There, you will also find cafes and antique stores. The best time to shop for antiques is on the third Saturday of the month when their flea-market (Mercantone dell' Antiquario) takes place.

Rome

Fendi and Valentino's flagship stores are located in Rome, as well other designers' boutiques. Most designer stores, as well as other shops, can be found in the area near Piazza di Spagna. Regular Romans shop in Via del Corso, between Piazza Venezia and Piazza del Popolo.

Rome is a good place to buy antique gold jewelry, artistic engraving in wood or metals, and of course, religious items.

The Roman flea market at Porta Portese in Trastevere is huge. (Bus #47 takes you there.) It is open on Sunday from 7 a.m. to 11 a.m. Besides antiques, you will also discover numerous other unique items. Wear comfortable walking shoes. (I didn't and ended up with blisters on my feet.)

Florence

The most popular shopping area for high-quality--although expensive--items in Florence are the streets in the Santa Maria Novella district. More affordable items can be found in the shops around Piazza della Repubblica. Besides its designer shops, Florence is famous for hand-crafted leather goods and artistic gold jewelry. Most leather stores are located on the streets around Piazza della Santa Crocce. Modern jewelry pieces can be found on Ponte Vecchio, the picturesque bridge that crosses the Arno River. The items found there are high quality and unique, but not necessarily a bargain. For antiques, head for Via Maggio, where several stores are located.

You can get some bargain leather and other items at Mercato Centrale, the market near Piazza Lorenzo and Mercato Nuovo near Piazza della Repubblica—just be careful that you're getting the real thing.

I bought a great red leather jacket at Mercato Centrale for a pittance, almost twenty years ago. I loved that jacket and it's still in excellent condition, but unfortunately, out of style. I'm keeping it just in case the puffy shoulders and baggy sleeves ever become fashionable again.

On Tuesdays, you'll find a colorful outdoor market in Parco delle Cascine where you can buy clothing, housewares, antiques and more.

In Florence, you can also get straw items, watercolor paintings and prints, decorative items made of leather, art work in carved wood or ceramics, and Tuscan pottery. I still have a wood carving of the Florence skyline, and a leather-covered flask I bought on my first visit to Florence over thirty years ago.

Venice

Venice is known for its glass objects, hand-made lace, and decorative masks. You can also purchase some interesting watercolors or prints.

The Mercerie & Calle Largo XXII Marzo, which run from Piazza San Marco (St. Mark's Square) to Rialto, is the main upscale shopping area. The streets from Rialto to Campo San Paolo are lined with less expensive stores.

The area of Lista di Spagna, near the train station going towards Rialto, sells inexpensive glass items, masks, and souvenirs. The markets are also located there. These areas are always swarming with tourists and day trippers.

Some of the items sold in the above location are run-of-the mill pieces for tourist consumption, especially the stuff sold at the outdoor stands; however, you may also come across some interesting items at reasonable prices. I have bought unusual glass jewelry, colorful vases, lovely watercolor paintings, and one very unique little leather purse there. If you're looking for some inexpensive T-shirts or sweatshirts to bring home to the children in your family, you will find them in that area. The markets even carry some extra-large sizes. Some of this inexpensive merchandise is surprisingly durable. I still have the Carnevale-themed sweat shirt I had to purchase one cold, wet April a couple of decades ago.

For higher quality and more unusual glass, take the ferry to Murano; for handmade lace, the place to go is Burano. It takes about twenty minutes to reach either of those locations by boat from Venice. For genuine, hand painted masks go to Tragicomico near Campo San Paolo, Leon d'Oro, or Mondonovo off Campo Santa Margherita. Stores will ship the items safely home to you, if you wish.

Naples Area

If you venture down South to the Naples area, you can find exquisite coral and cameos. You can also get beautiful hand-painted dishes from the Amalfi area.

The city of Faenza in the Emilia Romagna region is famous for its attractive, colorful glazed pottery called majolica. The regions of Tuscany and Umbria are also well-known for their pottery. The same items can also be found in stores selling housewares in other cities.

You will find ample shopping opportunities in all but the smallest cities of Italy, usually with prices lower than in the major metropolises. There are also new malls and outlets that have recently emerged in the suburbs. For up-to-date information, check the website of the cities you plan to visit or the local tourist office.

It used to be that Italian fashion was always a season ahead of ours, but recently there have been a few occasions where we've beaten them to the punch. Women in the U.S. were wearing capris and peasant skirts a year before the women in Italy, for example. Overall, though, the Italians are usually in the forefront of the fashion industry.

There used to be uniqueness about their designs that made shopping there exciting, but over the last decade many of their styles can be found in the States, although the craftsmanship is often better in Italy. I don't always find Italian styles appealing. The last time I was there, their upcoming winter line had a Russian influence and, although unique, I thought it was rather ugly. It reminded me of the Communist era.

Italian clothes worn by college students and teenagers have become quite Americanized--complete with the raggedy jeans and printed T-shirts. The last time I was in Italy, I tried to find a T-shirt with something Italian printed on it for one of the teenagers in our family, but had a difficult time; the writing on all of the shirts I saw was in English. I finally spotted one in a store similar to the many that line our malls in a mall in the suburbs of Trieste.

I love to look at the shoe store windows. Italian shoes and purses are unique and colorful, and there is always a large selection available. If you're shopping in the malls or department stores, check the labels to make sure the items are made of genuine leather and manufactured in Italy.

If you're planning to buy a bathing suit, think skimpy (and apply that to men's as well as women's swimsuits). One-piece bathing suits for women are a rarity, as are boxer-type trunks for men. (More on this subject in the Italian Way of Life section, p.136.)

Whatever you buy, whether it is clothes or shoes, try on a size larger than you would wear at home. If you're buying clothing for someone else, stick to sweaters or jerseys--something that will stretch, just in case.

Following are some important tips to ensure you get what you paid for when shopping in Italy:

Reputable shops will ship items to you for a fee.

It will take anywhere from a couple of weeks to three months for delivery, depending on how it is shipped. It's the easiest and safest way to send your purchases to the States. Pay with a credit card, if possible, so you'll be protected in case of a dispute, and ask the store to insure the items.

Beware of fakes. When buying locally-manufactured leather goods, designer items, or jewelry, make sure you are getting the real article. Although you can sometimes get a good deal at the markets, the traditional shops are a safer bet. This also applies to art work. You can purchase some charming watercolors done by local artists along the bridges and alleys of Venice, but make sure you get the real article and not some mass-produced garbage that looks like paint-by-number.

Do not buy any "designer" items from the street vendors who sell their wares from sheets spread out on the sidewalk, regardless of how "real" the item looks. There is a law against purchasing these counterfeit products. You could end up getting arrested and paying a hefty fine. Being a naïve tourist may save you from landing in jail, but won't keep you from being fined.

Go to the flea markets early and beware of pickpockets. The best items go fast, and pickpockets abound. You may find some great antiques, but unless you're an expert, stick to the traditional antiques stores.

Whatever liquid you buy, whether it's wine, olive oil or perfume, will have to be stored in your checked luggage unless you are flying directly from Italy to your final destination. This applies even to items purchased at the duty-free shops prior to departure. The bottle may be confiscated when you transfer from the plane you boarded in Italy to the one that will take you home. **This is true, despite what the duty-free shops tell you.** Your duty-free purchase may not even be safe from confiscation when you arrive at your final destination.

~

A couple of years ago, I flew home from Rome via Paris. Since my flight was direct from Paris to Pittsburgh, I bought a small bottle of raspberry brandy at the duty-free shop in the Paris airport. When I was screened prior to exiting the airport in Pittsburgh, TSA checked my carry-on and threatened to take my liqueur, but since it was barely over the three-ounce limit, they let me slide. This confused me, since I was headed home and not flying anywhere.

I asked my friend's son, who works for the TSA, the reason for the screening. He said it was probably because I was exiting in a restricted area, which still didn't make any sense to me, since I had already been amply screened when I boarded the plane in Paris, but...don't expect common sense from the TSA. Just beware!

On my return trips from Italy, I always bring back a bottle of liquor, as well as olive oil from my cousin Giordano's olive grove. I store them in plastic water bottles, tape the lids to ensure there's no leakage, wrap them in plastic, and place them in the middle of my suitcase. They have always arrived safely.

During the last trip, I spotted a large hole in the middle of my duffle bag when it arrived--three days after I did. I was afraid the airlines may have punctured my goodies and expected a disaster because besides the bottles, I was also carrying coffee for my mother, hot chocolate mix, and several pounds of candy. Surprisingly, they survived.

Some of my friends have stashed wine in its original glass bottle in their checked luggage, but I'm not that brave. So, if you're carrying liquids, I would recommend you transfer them to plastic bottles or cushion them well, and encase them in plastic.

WHAT YOU CAN BRING HOME

At the present time, you can purchase up to $800 worth of items duty-free, and you're limited to one quart of liquor. You can also bring 200 cigarettes and 100 cigars. Anything else is taxable. As a general rule, packaged items such as cookies or candy are allowed, as are certain types of hard cheeses and preserved meats. Check the U.S. Customs Service website for detailed, up-to-date information. Fruits, vegetables and perishable items are definitely not permitted. If you attempt to take them onto the plane, they will be confiscated.

After their first trip back to Italy, my mother and aunt wanted to bring home some of the scrumptious Viennese pastries for which Trieste is famous. They each bought a dozen of them, and showed up at the airport with the box of goodies in hand. When they went to check in, the airline clerk wanted to confiscate their pastries and "dispose" of them. "Nianche per sogno! (In your dreams!)" they said in unison. Then they sat down and consumed all of the goodies before boarding the plane. They felt slightly nauseated on the flight, but it was worth it.

TAXES

Italy has a value added tax called IVA on certain items. Non-European Union citizens can get a rebate if the total purchases total over 155 euros. It is a long, tedious process. Stores participating in the tax refund program should provide you with a form showing the tax paid. You will need to save the forms from all participating stores. Before you leave Italy, ask the customs officer at the airport to stamp the forms, and then present them to the refund office at the airport.

You must do this before you check your luggage because the customs' office may request to see the items listed, since the refund only applies to the items you're taking home. Global Refund is the main refund company. The other two are Premier Tax Free, and Euro Refund. You will either receive cash or the money will be credited to your credit card.

If you're planning to apply for a rebate, get to the airport early. This is a tedious, time-consuming process and, unless you've spent a lot of money, not worth the hassle. The other problem is that the customs' office and global refund office are only open during regular working hours, so if you have an early flight, you're out of luck. I attempted to do this on a couple of occasions, but decided it wasn't worth the aggravation and gave up.

All stores are required by law to give you a receipt and you are required to take it. Technically, you're supposed to keep it until you leave the country. I save the hotel receipts until I get home. **As for the ones for minor purchases, I keep them at least until I'm clear of the store. Not doing this could result in a fine.** A few stores in areas frequented by tourists have signs that advise the customer, in various languages, to keep the receipt.

Prices are shown differently than in America. Europeans use commas rather than periods to separate euros from cents. (50 euros 25 cents = 50,25); while they use periods to indicate thousands (2 thousand euros and 25 cents = 2.000,25). This can be confusing. My friend thought she had discovered a super bargain when she spotted a beautiful dress selling for a mere 5 euros; it was actually a designer dress worth 5000 euros.

STORE HOURS

Traditionally stores are open from 9 or 9:30 a.m. to 1:00 or 1:30 p.m., then from 4:00 or 4:30 p.m. until 7:00 or 7:30 p.m., and closed all day Sundays, Mondays, and holidays. This schedule applies to food shops, bakeries, as well as clothing sores. Lately, many supermarkets remain open continuously, but close at least one day a week.

During the last few years, some of the department stores have adopted the American way and are not taking their lunch break. They are open continuously, seven days a week. I've noticed changes every time I go, and with Italy's recent economic woes, things may continue to change. So, before you venture out shopping, get up-to-date information from your hotel. (For a list of shop types and Italian sizes, see the Appendix, p. 139.)

MAILING & SHIPPING

If you just need to buy stamps, you're better off purchasing them at a tobacco shop or magazine stand rather than wasting your time standing in line at the post office. Most tobacco shops sell stamps for overseas as well as for Italy. If the clerk doesn't speak English, ask for *francobolli per l'America*, or just point to the place in your letter or postcard where a stamp would go and say "America"; that's what I do when I'm in a country where I don't speak the language. **At the tobacco shop you can also buy batteries, bus tickets, phone cards, and of course, tobacco and matches.**

There are mailboxes throughout the city which are not always easy to spot since they are not large, free standing containers like ours, but small metal boxes attached to the outside of buildings. They are red and usually come in pairs. One will read *Per la Citta* (for the city); the other will read *Per Tutte le Altre Destinazioni* (for all other destinations). In some cases one may read *Poste per l'Italia* (mail for Italy) and the other *Poste per l'Estero* (foreign mail). In certain locations, there is one box with two slots. If you place your mail in the wrong box, it will eventually reach its destination, but it may take months. I accidentally dropped a postcard in the wrong box in August and my friend received it just before Thanksgiving.

If you decide to ship the items you purchased yourself, instead of relying on the store, you will need to go to a *cartoleria* (stationary shop) to buy a box, wrapping paper and tape, then stand in line at the post office. For prompt delivery, mail it *posta prioritaria* (priority mail). Insured valuables should be mailed *assicurata* (insured). Mailing items from Italy is not cheap and can be complicated, even if you speak Italian or they speak English. My most dreaded experience in Italy is when I have to deal with the post office.

Shipping items to and from Italy used to be simple nd relatively inexpensive, but over the last several years, that is no longer the case. The regulations have changed and the cost has increased. There are certain items you are not permitted to mail to Italy and the cost to mail acceptable items has increased. When shipping merchandise home from Italy, you no longer pay by exact weight, but by increments.

When I was spending a couple of months in Italy, I used to mail some of my clothes back and forth, but I have stopped doing this because of the hassle and expense involved. The first time I shipped my clothes, back in 2002, things went smoothly and the cost was reasonable. My package arrived in less than a month in both directions. Three years later, it was a whole different story.

I went to my local post office with my package wrapped and my customs' declaration form all filled out.

"I'm sorry, but you can't ship shoes into Italy," the clerk said, after reading my form. She sounded apologetic.

"They're not new shoes. They're my old shoes that I'm shipping to myself at my cousin's house. I shipped shoes the last time I went. When did the rule change?"

"I don't know when this went into effect...a lot of regulations changed since our government imposed higher taxes on Italian imports...the latest rule book says shoes are not permitted," the clerk said, pointing to a page in her manual

"That's insane. It's not like I'm shipping a dozen pairs of new shoes to sell. It's two pairs of old shoes I'm planning to wear."

"I know. It's stupid, but what can I say? I guess we have a lot of dumb regulations for items coming into the U.S. also."

I cursed our Congress, president, and anyone else who may have been involved, returned home, took the shoes out and replaced them with additional clothes, repacked the box, and finally mailed it along with a smaller package that, fortunately, did not include shoes. The cost of shipping had also increased considerably since the last time.

During my previous trip, my clothes had arrived in Italy in less than a month. On this occasion, I had allowed two months for delivery. My package showed up almost three months later—two weeks prior to my departure. Since I wasn't home at the time of delivery, I had to go pick up the package at the post-office, passport in hand, and lug it two miles uphill to my cousin's apartment where I was staying. The smaller package, which was a gift for a relative and sent directly to her, didn't reach her until after I had left, and she had to pay a tariff to get it.

Shipping things back home was even more fun. Along with my clothes, I also shipped some heavy books that I had purchased. I used the box in which my items had arrived, but still had to go to the "cartoleria" to get the proper tape and labels.

After taking a number and waiting in the usual post-office line holding a twenty-pound package, I was informed that it would cost me the equivalent of over $70 to mail it.

"Holy crap! Pesa pocco piu' di 10 kili. Come mai costa tanto? (It weighs a little over 10 kilos. How come it costs so much?)" I asked the clerk.

She explained to me that the rules had changed, and instead of the cost being based on the actual weight, it now increases by increments.

"Se puo' ridurre il peso a non piu'di dieci kili, costerebbe la meta. (If you can reduce the weight to no more than 10 kilos, it would cost you half as much.)" she said.

In other words, I was paying $35 for an excess of less than 2 pounds. I took the parcel to the park across the street from the post office, sat on a bench, carefully opened the package, and removed a heavy book that fortunately was on top. I resealed the box and returned to the post office. Of course, I had to wait in line again but I saved $35. It wasn't just because of the extra cost; it was the principle. I resented paying twice as much for a couple of pounds. That isn't the end of the story, though.

The carton arrived three months later. The box was torn and mangled, and there was a note of apology from my local post office stating they were not the ones who had abused my package. They had received it in that condition. The content had been rearranged. Nothing was missing, but the clothes on top felt damp and the pages of one of my books showed signs of having been exposed to water.

Since it had been raining on the east coast, I figured either the customs' agents or the Homeland Security people who had inspected my package must have left it out in the rain for quite a while for it to arrive in such a miserable condition. That was the last time I ever shipped anything in either direction. Now I bring less, buy less and take everything with me.

~

So, if you buy anything that you can't carry, let the store ship it, and if you're staying in Italy for a long period of time, you're better off paying for an extra suitcase, then shipping your excess clothes back and forth. Better yet, travel light, and do laundry more often.

LAUNDRY

The hotel laundry facility is the quickest way to take care of your dirty clothes without having to waste precious vacation time doing laundry. The cost can vary from dirt-cheap to outrageously expensive; however, you're taking a risk that the clothes will shrink, the colors will bleed, or your underwear will return as stiff as cardboard. I know people who have experienced all of the above, and cost was not an indicator of results.

~

My friends Angie and Mary Lou spent only 15 euros to have their laundry done at a Hotel Milano in Trieste, and their clothes returned clean, folded and fresh smelling. Another friend spent a small fortune to have her clothes washed in Florence, and her pants came back a size smaller. She thought they were tight because of all the pasta and gelato she had been eating until she realized the pants were also two inches shorter.

Just recently, my friend Mimi and her husband had their laundry done at a Pensione, and the clothes returned stiff and discolored.

~

If you decide to go to a laundromat, plan to spend a half day there because Italian washers and dryers, even the industrial ones, are much slower than ours. It takes almost two hours to wash and dry one load, although I've recently heard of a few places that have combination washer/dryers which work faster. Dry cleaners are also slow and expensive.

If I need to wash out a couple of items while traveling, I use the hotel sink or bidet. I roll the wet clothes in a towel to remove the excess water, and then hang them to dry in the shower. The little bottle of shampoo provided by the hotel makes a great laundry detergent. If the clothes are still damp in the morning, I finish drying them with the hairdryer. I also always carry a plastic bag in my suitcase in case I have to stick damp laundry in it. The bag also comes in handy to store wet shoes after getting caught in the rain.

SAFETY

Italy is a safe country if you use common sense. There's a strong police presence at all hours of the day and night, especially in the large cities. Besides the regular *polizia*, Italy has various other forces involved in law enforcement. If you find yourself in trouble, you can call on any of them for help. Just yell "*aiuto* (ah-you-tow)" loudly or "*polizia* (police-ia)" and some member of law enforcement will materialize. The emergency number for the police is 112; for a medical emergency it is 118.

Italian cities are as safe, if not safer, than most American ones provided you use common sense. You are unlikely to be a victim of violent crime, but there is a certain amount of petty theft, especially in the larger cities. There are fewer murders in Italy in a month, than we have in the city of Pittsburgh in a week; most of the homicides involve domestic disputes, (not innocent visitors). Drugs aren't as big of a problem as they are in the U.S. just yet. The mafia is still active in the south of Italy, but it doesn't usually bother tourists.

I have lived in Trieste, Italy and traveled throughout the country, but have never been robbed despite the fact that I'm not obsessed about safety. I just take the normal, common sense precautions. The key is to avoid being the victim of pickpockets and purse snatchers. Pickpockets are the scourge of the big cities, since you may not only encounter Italian thieves, but also criminals visiting from other countries. They steal wallets out of men's pockets and zoom past in their scooters, grabbing women's purses as the women walk along the sidewalk. Gypsies are also a problem; many of them are thieves in disguise. The minute you open your purse, your wallet will be gone.

Unfortunately, Americans are the primary targets of thieves because they believe we are all rich. **Below are some tips to keep your property safe:**
Don't advertise that you're an American. Leave the clunky tennis shoes at home. They immediately identify you as American because Italians and most other nationalities don't wear athletic shoes in the city. Get a pair of less conspicuous walking shoes.

If you're over thirty, don't wear any sweatshirts, jackets or hats with team or college logos. Besides the fact that Italians consider these items tacky, they scream "American," and the thieves can spot you at a distance. It's okay for young people to wear them because many European students wear American-style clothing.

Try to avoid walking around the crowded streets with your unfolded map in hand and camera equipment around your neck or wrist.

Keep your cash and documents in the hotel safe, if there is one. Just be sure to remember to remove them before you leave. An acquaintance of mine had to return to Rome from Florence because she had left money and passport in her hotel safe.

If no safe is available, find some other place to hide your valuables. I put part of mine in a dark plastic pouch, and hide it in the zippered part of my suitcase where the wheel gear is located, then lock my suitcase. It blends in so well, I often have a hard time finding it. I stash some cash and a copy of my documents in my dirty clothes bag.

My mother used to sew an extra pocket in the inside of the lining of her jacket. Of course, if you're like me, and sometimes forget your jacket on the backs of chairs, that's not a good place for your valuables. People have their own unique, creative ways to hide their cash.

Hide your money belts and avoid fanny packs. Get a lightweight money belt, and hide it under your clothes.

Although money belts are usually safe, some thieves have learned to quickly unbuckle them or even cut them. If you do wear one, be careful when you're surrounded by a crowd. Fanny packs give thieves easy access.

Watch your wallets and purses. Men: Don't keep your wallet in your backpack or back pocket. If you feel a hand caressing your posterior, whether it's attached to a male or female, it's probably someone trying to steal your wallet. I met a traveler who keeps an empty wallet in his pocket with a note to potential thieves.

Women: Keep your purse closed, and when walking, keep it on the inside of the sidewalk. Thieves on scooters speed by, close to the sidewalk, and attempt to grab your purse. This also applies to your cameras. Small bags, especially clutches, are hard to pick but easy to grab. A purse with a long strap is better. The strap should be placed across your chest, messenger-bag style, with the bag in the front. If your purse has a short handle, wrap the handle around your wrist and keep the purse in front of you. Don't ever sit your bag on the floor or hang it on the back of your chair in restaurants, especially if dining outdoors.

~

When I was staying at a hotel in Florence, a few years ago, an American woman told me about how her purse was stolen near the Duomo.

"We were sitting at an outdoor café having a beer," she said. "While my husband went to the bathroom, I stood up for a minute so I could get a better picture of the cathedral. When I sat back down, my purse was gone."

"Where did you leave it?" I asked, not that it mattered.

"It was on top of the table. I was only gone for a minute."

~

Thieves hang around touristy areas looking for such opportunities. Turning your back on your possessions, even for a second, is a mistake.

If strangers volunteer to take your picture, don't let them. It may be a way to get their hands on your camera.

~

While sitting in a café near the Trevi fountain during one of my very first trips to Italy, I watched a handsome young man ask a female tourist if he could take her picture. She smiled and promptly handed him her camera. As she posed in front of the fountain, he quickly disappeared in the crowd, along with her camera. It was a lesson learned.

So, when a man offered to take my picture, I was ready with a "No, thank you." He may have been just a fellow trying to be nice, but he may also have been a thief. I didn't want to find out which one.

~

Be careful with your possessions in any crowded area, even if the crowd consists of other Americans; our thieves travel, too. I found this out the hard way.

~

I'm sorry to say that the only time I had my purse picked was by American students. It didn't happen in Italy; it was in a train station in Niece, but it's still a valuable lesson.

At that time, each country used a different type of currency so I carried several wallets with various currencies. I was standing in line making train reservations and holding the wallet with the French francs in my hand. My small wallet, which contained Italian lire, a couple of travelers' checks, and a credit card, was in my purse that was hanging open on my shoulder.

I wasn't concerned because standing behind me was a group of young Americans with whom I had a brief conversation. I felt safe, and left my property unguarded. A few minutes later, when I stopped at the American Express office to cash my checks, my smaller wallet was gone.

I ran back to the station. I was madder than a raging bull and ready to confront the students, but they were gone. I only lost about $50 worth of lire, but the hassle of cancelling my credit card and replacing my checks stole a day from my brief vacation.

~

So, just because the strangers surrounding you are American and friendly, don't assume they're honest. Since then, I admit that on occasion I have left my luggage with American tourists while I went to the bathroom, but that was only in times of desperation, and after having a lengthy conversation that reassured me they wouldn't be absconding with my possessions.

Avoid aggressive beggars—especially gypsies with children. They will send their raggedy-looking toddlers to beg for money and, while you're handing them a dollar, the other children or their relatives will grab whatever they can. They hang around the train stations and other areas popular with tourists. They will surround you and attempt to rob you. Not all beggars are thieves, but if they're overly persistent or there's another party hanging around, assume they are, and be careful.

If you see a sudden commotion, stay away. It could be a ruse to distract potential victims. Thieves will sometime stage a diversion to attract your attention so their accomplices can pick your pockets or purse.

Don't leave luggage in your car. One of my former co-workers left his suitcases on a rack on top of his car, which was parked on a crowded street, while he checked into his hotel. When he returned to the car, his luggage was gone. Leaving suitcases on a luggage rack unattended was a dumb thing to do in any country.

Check your change. Learn the value of the euro coins and, when you purchase something or pay for tickets, make sure you get the right change. Count your money at the counter before you walk away. If you don't understand what the price is, ask the salesperson to write it down on a piece of paper. Italians write their numbers differently. They place a little mark on top of the 1, which sometime makes it look like a 7 and they cross the 7 to differentiate it from the 1.

Following is a good example of why you should check your change.

~

My brother Dan was in St Mark's Square in Venice; he was waiting in line to buy a ticket for the boat to the station. He watched as the person in front of him paid for a ticket, which cost 8.5 euros, with a 20 euro bill and noticed that when the clerk gave the man his change, he kept a 1 euro coin on the side of the window. The tourist took the change, stuffed it in his wallet without counting it, and walked away.

My brother suspected there was something shady going on, so he also paid for his ticket with 20 euros, and watched the clerk pull the same trick. Dan stood at the ticket booth, counted his change, and discovered he was 1 euro short.

"You owe me another euro," he said in Italian. He gave the clerk the type of glare he would give to one of his cheating students.

"Oh scusi, here it is," the clerk said, producing the coin. "I must have missed it."

"Yeah, right." my brother replied, rolling his eyes. As he was leaving, he said to the people in line: "Count your change because I think the clerk is a thief."

Avoid areas around train and bus stations after dark. That's where transients, derelicts and potential thieves often hang out.

I've outlined the potential situations where you may be vulnerable, but don't let the above scare you. With a few exceptions, I feel safer in most cities in Italy, even at night, than I do in my hometown of Pittsburgh these days. I've walked around alone after dark in many Italian cities and never felt threatened.

The difference is that if I'm careless in Italy, someone may try to take my wallet or purse, but they are not likely to hit me over the head or stick a gun in my back to get it. They will be swift and subtle.

LANGUAGE BARRIER

The language barrier is not much of an issue in Italy anymore. Most Italians, especially those who deal with tourists, speak an adequate amount of English. The majority of people under the age of fifty have studied it in school, and Italians are exposed to it via movies, television and especially computers. Airports, train and bus stations in major cities usually employ English-speaking people. But, don't assume everyone does.

In a shop or restaurant, ask politely if the clerk or waiter speaks English, don't expect that they should. Remember, even though English is the international language, you're in a country that is not your own.

I once witnessed an unpleasant scene in a small town where an American tried to buy some cookies.

"How much is a pound of those cookies?" the lady asked in a Southern accent, pointing to the display case.

"Scusi, non comprendo, (Sorry, I don't understand)" the clerk said politely.

"Those there cookies, how much?" the woman said, in a loud tone. She appeared irritated.

I got up from the little table where I was enjoying a cream-filled pastry, and tried to help the lady. "I speak Italian. I can help you."

"Oh thank you honey. I can't believe these people don't speak English," she ranted. She seemed visibly annoyed.

"She's older," I said, referring to the saleswoman. "They weren't teaching English in school when she was young."

"Well, she shouldn't be waiting on people if she doesn't speak English." This customer was indignant.

"This is Italy, not the U.S.," I said. I was having difficulty hiding my annoyance. "How many shop keepers in the U. S. do you know who speak Italian, or any other foreign language, for that matter?" I said.

The woman stared at me with a puzzled look on her face. I wasn't sure if my comment made her realize how absurd her expectations were.

I ordered the cookies, and apologized to the clerk for the woman's ignorant behavior. I gave the elderly clerk a friendly smile and said a polite "arrivederci" as I left.

~

Unfortunately, it wasn't the first or last time I've had to apologize for the rude behavior of our countrymen. So, please try to be conscientious in your actions; remember, you are representing the United States. Speaking loudly is not going to get Italian-speakers to understand. Ask if anyone in the establishment speaks English; if they do not, point and use sign language. You'd be surprised by how well you can communicate.

If you do find someone who speaks English, speak to them slowly in proper, simple English, and use common, easily understood words. Don't be tempted to use slang, abbreviations, or regional terminology. The only places you might run into a serious language problem is in small, remote towns, where most people only speak the local dialect. I'm fluent in Italian, but when I went to Sicily, I sometime had difficulty communicating. Their dialect is so far removed from the Italian language; they may as well have been speaking Greek. Even when they spoke the proper Italian, their accent was difficult to understand. Some of the dialects spoken in the small mountain villages of Northern Italy are also difficult to comprehend.

Learn a few basic words to help you survive. Quite often common sense can help you figure out the language, and if you've studied a few semesters of Spanish or French, you should be able to manage quite well, especially in Venice where the dialect has a lot of Spanish influences. Some Italian words are easy to decipher since they're similar to English. Be careful, though, because sometimes they are not what you think (i.e. a *libreria* is not a library, but a book store). I've made mistakes also, which provided my relatives with some laughs.

~

I was explaining to my Italian cousin about my allergy to certain preservatives and I used the word "preservativi," which I assumed was Italian for preservatives. I told her about how I have to read every label to make sure there aren't any offending preservatives in the food.

She gave me a puzzled look. "Cosa cerchi di dirmi? (What are you trying to tell me?)" she asked.

"You know! Preservativi--the stuff they put in food to keep it from spoiling."

She couldn't stop laughing. "I hope you didn't tell anyone else that," she said, still chuckling. Preservativi is something men use for birth control (condoms); the word you're looking for is conservanti. For a minute there you had me thinking American producers were putting birth control substances in your food," she said, still laughing.

ETIQUETTE & THE ITALIAN WAY OF LIFE

Courtesy is extremely important to the Europeans, especially the Italians. When entering and leaving an establishment, it is customary to greet the people with a general *buongiorno* (good day) or *buona sera* (good evening). You can also use *arrivederci* (I'll see you) upon leaving. If you feel uncomfortable trying the Italian, you should at least greet them in English. The clerk or waiter will usually approach you with: *"Prego, signor (or signora)"* and ask if you need help (*posso auitarla*) or escort to your seat. If you just want to browse, ask permission to look (*posso guardare*) before you start handling things.

In antique stores or other shops selling fragile items, you may see a sign that states *vietato toccare* (forbidden to touch) or something a little more polite that basically tells you to keep your paws off of the merchandise. I recently saw a sign in a Venice shop which read: *"Se lo rompi; lo compri."* (if you break it; you buy it). They mean it, so don't touch. If you see a sign on a shelf with something written on it besides the price, assume you can't touch the merchandise. That's my policy when I go into a country where I don't speak the language. I learned this after a rather large woman was ready to break my arm when I picked up a clock in an antique shop in Germany.

If you need to ask someone for directions or other information, start the conversation with *scusi*, (excuse me) before you proceed with your request. There are two other important words you should learn: *prego* (please; you're welcome) and *grazie* (thank you). I have to admit that it normally takes me a couple of days to remember to greet the clientele as I enter a store. By the time I leave, though, the greeting becomes a habit which I carry back to the States. I love the puzzled expression on the face of the clerks in the U.S. when I automatically greet them—in Italian—as I enter.

Italians are sociable people, so in certain places and situations, they may share a table with you at a restaurant, especially when you're alone. They love their *aperitivi*, wines, and liqueurs, but **they frown upon public drunkenness**. If you get visibly intoxicated in a bar or restaurant, you will be asked to leave. Don't resist or become disruptive unless you want to land in jail.

SOCIAL PRACTICES

Smoking is generally forbidden in public places, but a few restaurants and bars have smoking areas. Smoking is sometime permitted in the outdoor areas of cafes and restaurants. Most trains still have smoking and non-smoking compartments, although during my last trip, I noticed that the smoking cars had been eliminated from some of the short-distance trains. There are plenty of tobacco shops around the cities where cigarettes can be purchased. Matches are not distributed free with cigarettes; you have to pay for them.

Picking your teeth in public after dinner is acceptable and customary. In fact, toothpicks are provided for that purpose.

Men often call each other by their last name (without the "mister"), especially on the job; **women use their maiden names for all legal matters**, and most use it professionally regardless of their occupation.

Women breastfeed in public—anytime, anywhere, except maybe in church.

Contrary to popular myth, men do not pinch women in the butt--at least I've never seen it or experienced it. You may find someone who tries to invade your personal space on a crowded bus or train, though. Sometimes it's unavoidable, but if you suspect that the "space invader" is looking for a fast thrill or trying to get close to your wallet, a quick jab with the elbow is appropriate.

Some young men still whistle or comment on a woman's appearance, especially if she's alone and they are in a group. They often attempt to "pick-up" foreign women, and sometime follow them around town. Don't be concerned; the men are usually harmless, but they can sometimes be annoying.

~

During one of my first visits to Italy, when I was young, there were men trying to pick me up every time I went out alone, despite the fact that I was not a candidate for Miss America. I hadn't learned how to "dress and act Italian" then, so they immediately spotted me as a foreigner.

At first, the attention was good for my ego, but after a while it became annoying since some were rather persistent. One actually followed me all the way to my hotel and waited in the lobby for me, despite the fact that I had told him I was going to have dinner with my relatives. I had to sneak out via the back door, wearing a scarf and sunglasses.

One young man I met seemed rather disappointed when he found out I wasn't—as he put it—"a real American." I asked him why American girls are so popular in Italy.

"American women are always interested in romance with Italian men," he said.

"Not always," I thought to myself.

~

I had similar problems when I took my then sixteen-year-old niece with me, in the late 1980's. Young, and even not-so-young, men were flirting with her, and trying to pick her up despite the fact that I was with her. Fortunately, she had a steady boyfriend at home and wasn't interested. A friend's college-aged daughter, who was recently in Italy on a school trip, told me there were plenty of young men willing to "show her a good time." Apparently, things haven't changed with the new millennium; Italian men are still pursuing women, sometimes with humorous results.

~

A few years ago, I was dressed in jeans and a sweater and walking alone through the streets of Lucca. I *was busy perusing my map, and hadn't noticed that some young men had appeared out of nowhere and were walking behind me. The young Lotharios started making comments.*

"Hey bella, where are you going?" one yelled in Italian.

"You look really good in those jeans," the other one added. "Come have some coffee with us."

At first, I didn't pay any attention to them assuming they were talking to some young lady. I was walking slowly, head bent, studying my map, and didn't see anyone else approaching. The comments continued, so I turned around and was surprised to realize they were actually talking to me.

The look on their faces when they discovered that I was probably old enough to be their grandmother was priceless.

"Oh scusi, Signora," one of them said in an apologetic tone. They looked embarrassed.

"That's okay boys," I said. "Thanks for the compliment."

That made my day. It was nice to know I still attracted male attention—at least from behind.

~

Italian women are also interested in meeting American men, but they are not as aggressive as their male counterparts. They go about it in a more subtle, casual way. They smile and flirt without being overt.

While on the subject of social customs, it's worth mentioning that it's not unusual in Italy for men to carry purses and women to walk arm in arm. If you see a man carrying a shoulder bag, or two women walking arm-in-arm or holding hands, it does not mean they are gay.

Some men carry messenger-style satchels worn on their shoulders. They have been doing this since the 1960's, probably because their tight pants don't allow room for a wallet or keys. Ladies, especially older ones, often walk arm-in-arm when taking their *passegiata* (stroll), while younger women sometimes hold hands. The custom of walking arm-in-arm started as a way for women to steady each other while walking on the cobblestoned streets; the hand-holding is a sign of friendship that began when the women were little girls and often continues into adulthood.

~

I never thought much about the above customs until I traveled to Italy with my friend Gerry, who happened to be from Minneapolis.

"You sure have a lot of gay people in Italy," she said. "...and old ones, too," she added as she glanced around the streets of Rome.

"What do you mean? How do you know who is gay?" I said, with a puzzled look on my face.

"All those guys in the tight clothes and purses...and those ladies walking arm in arm, aren't they gay?"

I couldn't stop laughing. She must have thought half the population of Italy was gay.

~

DRESS CODE & CUSTOMS

Proper dress is required for visits to churches and especially the Vatican. Shorts and mini-skirts are forbidden, and women must keep their upper torso and arms covered. Some of the smaller churches may be more lenient, but if you're planning to visit any important cathedral, it's safer **to dress appropriately so you don't risk being denied entry.**

Italians take pride in their appearance and believe in propriety. In the cities, they are smartly dressed and fashionable. You will not find sweat suits, sagging jeans, or sloppy clothes on anyone over thirty. Neither sex wears shorts downtown, or into restaurants or bars. In the summer, women wear mostly skirts or dresses. Students, however, are interchangeable with ours since they dress basically the same.

Italians' conservative street attire is a sharp contrast to what they wear to the beach. They are sun worshippers. They hit the beach at the first hint of spring, and swim until the middle of October, if weather permits. I sometime wonder if they ever heard of melanoma and other evils of the sun because they try to soak up as much of it on their bodies as is legally possible. People dress much more scantily at the beach than they do in the U.S., regardless of their age or shape. Women wear tiny bikinis; men sport tight Speedos that show off their wares, and topless sunbathing is permitted on most Italian beaches.

During my visit in 2010, my relatives informed me that going topless on public beaches is now out of fashion. The news must not have reached everyone because I saw plenty of topless bathers, although I admit many were not speaking Italian. I surmised they were part of the Northern Europeans who converge on the southern beaches every summer. I noticed a different protocol among the nationalities. Most Italian women will sun-bathe topless, but cover-up when they enter the water or go to the refreshment stand, while foreigners will strut their stuff everywhere, regardless of their shape, size or age. What makes this particularly interesting is that many beaches are located off of main roads, and since the refreshment stands and other facilities are often on the sidewalk, anyone driving past can see some sights which in the States would cause major traffic jams.

I've encountered very few Americans on European beaches, but if they're topless, they are easy to identify— they're the ones with the burned breasts. I have never had the courage to go topless, even in my younger days. Even if I could have overcome my puritanical upbringing, I always feared there'd be an international incident at the beach, and I would find myself on CNN with electronic pasties covering my breasts. I have to admit, though, that it must be liberating to be able to let it all hang out without any inhibitions. Since it is part of the culture, it becomes the norm. What's appropriate attire in the States may attract attention in Italy.

~

During one of my last visits to a beach in Trieste, my ultra-conservative one-piece bathing suit attracted more stares than if I had been naked. I usually go to the Lanterna, an old, segregated beach where men and women swim on separate sides of a seven-foot wall and the majority of the women, many of whom are senior citizens, go topless. Most of the ladies were so tan that they could easily have passed for Africans. With my lily-white body and one-piece swim suit, I stood out like an albino monkey. The fact that I was also wearing rubber beach shoes made me even more of a misfit. I noticed several women furtively looking at me as I worked my way into the water.

After my swim, I sat down and opened my Newsweek, which I hadn't finished reading at home. If the beach shoes and bathing suit hadn't been enough of a sign that I wasn't a local, my magazine confirmed it. There were two very-tan, topless ladies in their mid-fifties sitting on a blanket next to me. One of them was wearing a thong bottom. Through my peripheral vision, I could see they were checking me out.

I sensed that they were about to comment on my attire, so I made the quick decision to let them know that I spoke Italian before they said something that might have embarrassed them and annoyed me.

"How do you Triestines manage to walk on those stones so gracefully without falling?" I asked in a mixture of Italian and the local dialect.

"We've been doing it since we were kids. We've developed calluses on the bottom of our feet," one of them replied. "Aren't you hot in that severe bathing suit?" the woman in the thong asked.

"I'm used to it. That's the way women of a certain age dress for the beach where I live."

"Where is that?"

"Pittsburgh, Pennsylvania, U.S.A."

"In America? I thought people were even more naked than us on American beaches...we see all those pictures of movie stars."

"Those are probably taken on their private property...or your European beaches. There are a few nude beaches in the U.S. and nudist camps, but if I went on a public beach wearing as little as you ladies, I'd get arrested for indecent exposure."

"You're kidding?! I didn't realize they were so conservative over there. It's a shame. The sun is good for you."

I didn't want to tell them how we've been indoctrinated to believe that the sun is our evil enemy and we should avoid it at all costs.

"Well, you're here now. You should at least get a two-piece

bathing suit. You'll feel a lot cooler," one of the women suggested.
Another topless friend joined them, interrupting the conversation. She was a skinny woman in her late fifties; she had long, pointy breasts that reminded me of tube socks and hung far too low to go unsupported. It made me appreciate the benefits of clothes.

The next day, I dug out my old, black, one-piece bathing suit with the mesh middle that I store at my cousin's apartment. It gave the illusion of being a two-piece, while still containing my belly. The suit is ten-years old and bit snug, so I only wear it in Italy.

I didn't feel as conspicuous on the beach that day, but a funny thing happened: a couple of other senior citizens were wearing one-piece suits and by the time August was over, there were several more.

I think I might have started a new trend. I guess those women discovered certain bodies looked better covered.

~

On the subject of nudity, don't be surprised if you see billboards or posters featuring half-naked women advertising soap or body products, and similar ads on television. At first, I was shocked by all this exposure, especially since Italy is a Catholic country; but after spending a few weeks there, I no longer noticed it.

As my friend Janice's twelve-year old nephew told his buddy when asked how he liked the topless beaches in Europe: "No big deal.. After you've seen so many boobs, it's like looking at elbows."

MISCELLANEOUS INFORMATION

Italy's time is six hours ahead of Eastern Standard Time. They observe daylight saving time, which starts in March and ends in October. Military time is used in Italy (i.e. 3 p.m. = 15:00 hr.)
The dates are shown as day, month, year (i.e. April 3, 2012 = 3-4-2012).The days of the week on a calendar start with Monday.

I hope the information provided in this guide will help assure smooth sailing on your Italian adventure.

HAVE A GREAT TRIP!

APPENDIX

ITALIAN LEGAL HOLIDAYS:

New Year's Day – January 1
Easter Monday
Liberation Day – April 25
Labor Day – May 1
Assumption of the Virgin (Ferragosto) – August 15
All Saints' Day – November 1
Feast of the Immaculate Conception – December 8
Christmas Day – December 25
St. Stephen's Day – December 26

Cities also celebrate the feast of their patron saint:
Venice – St. Mark – April 25
Florence – St. John the Baptist – June 24
Rome – Sts. Peter and Paul – June 29

If the holidays fall on a Thursday or Tuesday, establishments often create a long weekend by closing on the Friday or Monday. They call it "fare il ponte" (make a bridge).

MONTHS OF THE YEAR:

Gennaio – January
Febbraio – February
Marzo – March
Aprile – April
Maggio – May
Giugno – June
Luglio – July
Agosto – August
Settembre – September
Ottobre – October
Novembre – November
Dicembre – December

DAYS OF THE WEEK:

Lunedi -- Monday
Martedi - Tuesday
Mercoledi - Wednesday
Giovedi -- Thursday
Venerdi -- Friday
Sabato -- Saturday
Domenica – Sunday

TYPES OF SHOPS

Antique – Antiquario
Bakery – Panetteria, panificio (sells just bread, or bread and pastries)
Bookstore – Libreria
Butcher – Macelerria
Clothing Store – Negozio di Abbigliamento, Botique
    (for: women – feminile; men – maschile; children – per bambini)
Deli – Salumeria
Department Store – Grande Magazzino
Drugstore – Drogheria (does not sell drugs – just other drug store items (not food).
Fish Market – Pescheria
Fruit & Vegetable Market – Fruttivendolo,
General Grocery Store – Alimentari (usually doesn't sell paper products)
Hairdresser – Parucchiere
Jewelry Store -- Gioielleria
Ice Cream Parlor – Gelateria
Newsstand – Edicola
Pastry Shop – Pasticerria (some sell just pastries; some also sell bread)
Pharmacy – Farmacia (drugs and related items only)
Post Office - Posta
Shoe Store – Negozio di Scarpe (Shoes and purses only)
Supermarket – Supermercato
Tobacco Shop – Tabacceria (also sells stamps, batteries, bus tickets, phone cards)
Travel Agency – Agenzia di Viaggi

SIZES

(*Taglia*) – for clothes; (*Misura*) – for shoes.

Women's dresses and skirts:

American 4   6   8   10   12   14   16   18
Italian   36 38 40 42   44   46   48   50

Women's Shoes:

American 5   6   7   8   9   10
Italian   36 37 38 39 40 41

Men's Suits:

American 34 36 38 39 40 41 (inches)
Italian   44 46 48 50 52 56 (size)

Men's Shirts (based on collar size):

American 14 15 16 17 18 (inches)
Italian   44 46 48 50 52 (size)

Men's shoes:

American 7   8   9   10 11 12
Italian   39 41 43 44 46 48

Small – *Piccolo (piccolo)*

Medium – *Medio (media)*
L)arge – *Grande or Larga*

Some clothes labels show both European and American sizes.

USEFUL WORDS & PHRASES:

Good Day (Hello) – Buongiorno
Good Evening – Buona Sera
Goodbye – Arrivederci

Thank you – Grazie
Please – Prego
Excuse me – Scusi
I'm sorry – Mi dispiace

Hour – Ora
Day – Giorno
Week – Settimana
Month – Mese
Year – Anno
Today – Oggi
Yesterday – Ieri
Tomorrow – Domani

Toilet – Gabinetto
Men – Uomini, Signori
Women – Donne, Signore

I don't understand Italian – Non capisco Italiano
I don't speak – Non parlo
Where is ... – Dov'e...

Made in United States
North Haven, CT
28 February 2023